Jenni's creativity, wit, warmth, and open a[...]
journey forever set the bar high as an exam[...]
recovery. NEDA has strongly recommende[...]
ten years, and we believe it will have a long s[...] for many more.

—Lynn S. Grefe, President and CEO,
National Eating Disorders Association (NEDA)

Life Without Ed is an essential resource for any recovering person and for those who work with eating disorders. People tell me again and again how much *Life Without Ed* has mattered to them. Its practical, hands-on approach gives readers a clear idea of the specific, day-to-day actions they can take toward health.

—Marya Hornbacher, award-winning journalist and
bestselling author of Wasted; Madness; Sane; *and* Waiting

Life Without Ed's uplifting intimate inner dialogue has energized countless young women—and men—in their own recoveries from eating disorders.

—Leigh Cohn, coeditor,
Current Findings on Males with Eating Disorders

Of all the great books written on eating disorders, none has had a wider reach than *Life Without Ed.* Those suffering have found connection and hope; family members have found understanding and empathy; professionals have learned from it and praised it. It will remain a classic for decades to come.

—Michael E. Berrett, PhD, cofounder, Center for Change; coauthor,
Spiritual Approaches in the Treatment of Women with Eating Disorders

In our work with couples, *Life Without Ed* has become required reading for partners of people with eating disorders. Jenni's honest narrative is the perfect tool to help partners learn to separate out the disorder from their loved one. It builds empathy, gives hope, and helps restore relationships.

—Cynthia M. Bulik, PhD, Director, UNC Center of Excellence
for Eating Disorders; author, Midlife Eating Disorders

Life Without Ed stands out as a pivotal contribution to the eating disorder field. Jenni's detailed account of her own recovery, and her quest to help others on a similar journey, broke through barriers, speaking directly to sufferers and their loved ones, and continues to inspire people all over the world. Jenni and *Life Without Ed* have become legendary examples that one should never give up hope.

—Carolyn Costin, LMFT, Executive Director, Monte Nido
and Affiliates; author, The Eating Disorder Sourcebook
and 8 Keys to Recovery from an Eating Disorder

Life Without Ed is the first book I give to clients when they walk in the door. An intelligent, compassionate guide down the road to recovery.
—*Wendy Oliver-Pyatt, MD, author,* Fed Up!

Life Without Ed is literally a lifesaver—empowering recovery, shedding light on the darkness of these illnesses, and inspiring hope and connection to a life outside the prison of an eating disorder.
—*Margo Maine, PhD, author,* The Body Myth; Father Hunger; *and* Body Wars

Jenni is truly a remarkable woman. She unselfishly shares her struggles and triumphs. Her candid and inspiring story will help those suffering from their own "Ed." I feel privileged to know her and her story.
—*Jamie-Lynn Sigler, actress*

Life Without Ed is on my list of top recommended books! Easy to read, insightful, and full of fantastic advice.
—*Susan Albers, PsyD, author,* Eating Mindfully

Life Without Ed is the only book for sufferers that I recommended to my daughter during her illness. An engaging, practical, and positive approach to recovery . . . for people with eating disorders and for those who love them!
—*Laura Collins, author,* Eating with Your Anorexic

After reading *Life Without Ed*, I began the process of believing in myself again, fighting back against "Ed," and, ultimately, living a recovered life. As a male who struggled with an eating disorder for several years, I can say without hesitation that *Life Without Ed* is an invaluable resource for individuals of both genders and all backgrounds.
—*Adam Lamparello, author,* Ten-Mile Morning

One decade later, this inspirational and practical book still stands out among the many in the how-I-overcame-my-eating-disorder genre. In particular, the author separates out the dysfunctional eating disorder voice (that she calls "Ed") from Self. This simple step is the beginning of healing, which also helps to dampen a person's profound guilt with eating behaviors and body shame. The short chapters are written with wit and compassion.
—*Evelyn Tribole, MS, RD, coauthor,* Intuitive Eating

Life Without Ed has been an important resource for the past decade for sufferers and families affected by eating disorders. It gave them a language to better understand and share their experiences about these devastating illnesses. Just as importantly, it launched Jenni as a figure of inspiration for so many by living the example that full recovery is indeed possible.
—*Ovidio Bermudez, MD, Chief Medical Officer, Eating Recovery Center*

Life Without Ed

TENTH ANNIVERSARY EDITION

JENNI SCHAEFER

with THOM RUTLEDGE, LCSW

Mc
Graw
Hill
Education

New York   Chicago   San Francisco   Athens   London   Madrid
Mexico City   Milan   New Delhi   Singapore   Sydney   Toronto

37 38 39 40 41 42   LCR   25 24 23 22 21 20

ISBN   978-0-07-142298-7
MHID   0-07-142298-6

e-ISBN 978-0-07-183423-0
e-MHID   0-07-183423-0

Library of Congress Cataloging-in-Publication Data

Schaefer, Jenni.
        Life without Ed : How One Woman Declared Independence from Her Eating
Disorder and How You Can Too / Jenni Schaefer.
             p.   cm.
        ISBN 0-07-142298-6
          1. Schaefer, Jenni—Health.   2. Eating disorders—Patients—Biography.
      3. Eating disorders—Treatment—Case studies.   I. Title.

      RC552.E18 S345   2004
      616.85'26'0092—dc22   2003015118

McGraw-Hill Education products are available at special quantity discounts to use as premiums and sales promotions, or for use in corporate training programs. To contact a representative, please visit the Contact Us pages at www.mhprofessional.com.

This book provides a variety of ideas and suggestions. It is sold with the understanding that the publisher and author are not rendering psychological, medical, or professional services. The author is not a doctor or psychologist, and the information in this book is the author's own opinion, unless otherwise stated. The information contained in this book is intended to provide helpful and informative material on eating disorders. It is not intended to serve as a replacement for professional medical or psychological advice. All medical, dietetic, or therapeutic recommendations mentioned in this book are not meant to be taken without the advice of a medical doctor, registered dietician, and/or licensed therapist.

To protect anonymity, the names of some of the people mentioned in this book have been changed, as have certain descriptive details. Also, to ensure privacy, some of the events and characters are composites of several individual events or persons.

As with the original edition of *Life Without Ed*, this book

is *still* dedicated to my amazing mom and dad,

Susan and Joe Schaefer

Contents

3

Mirror, Mirror on the Wall — *Is Thin Really Everything?*   *61*

6

The Hard Truth — *Getting Serious About Getting Better   141*

7

Believe It — *What It's All About   171*

Afterword —— *Ten Years Later*   *187*

Acknowledgments

I WANT TO THANK everyone who helped me walk the most difficult road of my life and then stood by my side as I wrote a book about it.

This book is dedicated to my mom and dad. Thank you for your unconditional love and support throughout my life. I am so lucky to have you as parents.

I express my deep gratitude to my older brother, Steve Schaefer, and his wife, Destiny. You are always there for me when I need you. To my little brother, Jeffery Schaefer, thank you for your humor, ever-present encouragement, and uplifting perspective on life.

This book would not exist without three people. Thank you to Thom Rutledge for making recovery such a fun journey, for encouraging me to write a book and giving me guidance all along the way, and for your important contributions to *Life Without Ed*. I greatly appreciate my agent, Adam Chromy, and his enthusiasm for my project and belief in me. To my editor, Michele Matrisciani, thank you for your expert assistance and for seeing something special in my book from the very beginning.

Thank you to all of the health care professionals who helped me along the road to recovery: Dr. A. Lee Tucker, Dr. Ovidio Bermudez, Dr. Brian Swenson, and "Susan" (Reba Sloan and Carol Beck).

I would never have been able to divorce Ed without Judy Rodman and Emily Lowe. Judy, thanks for being there for me with love, truth, and wisdom no matter where I am. And Emily, I will never forget how you stood by my side and always encouraged me to do the next right thing for my recovery.

Thank you to all of my friends and family back home in Texas. Even though you could not physically be with me as I fought Ed, you were always just a phone call away and helped me through many challenging times.

And to the amazing women in the Monday night Parkwest eating disorder therapy group, so much of this book was inspired by you. Keep taking recovery one day at a time and find the freedom that you deserve in a life without Ed.

Update for the Tenth Anniversary Edition

Life Without Ed was "the little engine that could," or so I have been told by several who work in book publishing. Not originally envisioned as a bestseller, but with grassroots support from devoted readers over the years, this little train finally made it to the top of the hill. And by that, I mean that *Life Without Ed* found its way into people's hearts. An author couldn't ask for more. This never would have happened without the incredible outpouring of encouragement and love that I have received from people in the eating disorders field. From professionals who specialize in eating disorders to those who work in advocacy and education to individuals touched personally by the illness, thanks for believing in me—from the very beginning.

This anniversary edition certainly would not exist without Kathryn Keil, my amazing editor at McGraw-Hill. Thanks, Kathy, for being so enthusiastic about all of my ideas even when they sometimes changed moment to moment! And Ann Pryor, you—I am grateful—were there when *Life Without Ed* first got pushed out onto those railroad tracks. To others at McGraw-Hill, especially Christopher Brown, Stacey Ashton, Susan Moore, and Laura Yieh, I appreciate both your expertise and wholehearted support. Thanks also to Linda Loewenthal at David Black Agency for your great wisdom and belief in my work.

Special words of appreciation go out to my friend and clinical psychologist Michael E. Berrett for providing just the insight that I needed to get in touch with my heart about the writing process for this edition. And to another friend and clinical psychologist, Jennifer J. Thomas, your feedback has been invaluable. Additional thanks to Eric Fluhr, Meg Burton, Jessica Meltzer, Susie Hair, Wynde Pustejovsky, and Amy Pettengill, who all shared their unique perspectives, excitement, and love. To Adam Lamparello, Vic Avon, Troy Roness, and Michael Elmer: you guys are simply the best. I appreciate your sharing your stories with me—not to mention, the world.

Many thanks to Dr. Phil McGraw, Anthony Haskins, Justin Arluck, and the rest of the "Dr. Phil" staff, who have supported my books as well as pointed millions of people in the direction of help and recovery.

And to Lynn Grefe and all of the staff at the National Eating Disorders Association (NEDA), it is you who people reach out to when they decide to get help. Thanks for answering all of the calls and for standing behind what I do. To Susie Roman, Maggi Flaherty, and Ellen Domingos, it has been an honor to participate in your wonderful programs over the years.

I also want to acknowledge everyone who has ever invited me to speak at an event. Because of you, I have been able to connect face-to-face with people who have read my books, which has deeply enriched both my personal and professional life.

You, the reader, are why I am able to do what I do. Thanks is not enough.

Everyone listed here is part of the engine that pulled *Life Without Ed* up that hill. I would have included more names, but the truth is that I had a limited amount of room in the book for the acknowledgements. So my words here may not be perfect, but you taught me that being perfect doesn't matter. Thanks for that, too.

Foreword

THE FIRST NIGHT I met Jenni Schaefer she ripped a floor pillow to pieces. The cotton stuffing was everywhere, the fabric all over the group therapy room, and Jenni looked quite relieved.

She was talking about her eating disorder and everything it had stolen from her.

"What are you feeling right now?" I asked Jenni.

"Mad," she answered simply.

"Describe what mad feels like," I said.

As Jenni searched for the right words, I noticed something more important than words. As she spoke, her hands clenched and unclenched like she was squeezing something in the air.

"What do you feel in your hands?" I asked. "There seems to be a lot of energy there."

Jenni paused as her concentration shifted to her hands that were now two tight fists. "Angry, very angry," she said.

"What do your hands want to do?"

"Rip something up," Jenni answered so quickly that she surprised even herself.

A few minutes later, a perfectly good floor pillow had given its life so that Jenni might begin her journey to recovery.

Jenni dove headfirst into the work of recovery from her eating disorder. My clients don't usually do something as courageous on their first night in group therapy as destroying part of the office decor. But that first night, Jenni was ready; Jenni was determined.

Determination does not guarantee an excellent recovery. The road ahead of Jenni was not particularly smooth. She would stumble and fall on her face—and on her butt—many times along the way. But I could always see her determination. Jenni lost sight of it from time to time, but I never did. This young woman was committed to staying on the recovery path and not looking back.

My work with Jenni has always been enjoyable. She made my job so much easier because she worked so hard. She was constantly taking notes during her sessions, but somehow her note taking never distracted from the work. Although she described her notebook as her own personalized self-help book, the idea of writing a book about eating disorder recovery did not occur to her for some time. She was in Nashville to pursue her dream of performing and songwriting after all.

Now I know that those therapy notes have paid off—not just for Jenni, but for you too.

You hold in your hands an extremely practical book. If you are struggling with an eating disorder, *Life Without Ed* can show you the way out. If you love someone with an eating disorder, *Life Without Ed* can help you make sense of what has previously been beyond comprehension. And if you are a mental health professional, *Life Without Ed* can take you inside the mind of a person with an eating disorder and teach you more than any research paper ever could about how to treat this insidious illness.

Life Without Ed is like no other book about eating disorder recovery. It has two important features that are missing from most books on the subject. First, it is simultaneously hopeful and realistic. Because having an eating disorder is such a frustrating experience (major understatement), these two elements do not coexist easily. Jenni shares her experiences in ways that acknowledge the nuts-and-bolts difficulties of recovery, while remaining the beam of hope that tells readers by her example, "If I can do this, so can you." And for those of you currently thinking that other people can recover from eating disorders but you can't, I am here to tell you that Jenni Schaefer absolutely believed the very same thing not so very long ago.

Beyond practical, realistic, and hopeful, *Life Without Ed* has another very important element that has been only hinted at in other eating disorder books: humor.

In our all-or-none, black-or-white culture, humor about eating disorders has either not existed or it has been tasteless and abusive, implying that this is a condition brought on by extreme vanity and that those who have eating disorders are shallow and vacant of real values. Nothing could be further from the truth. The people with eating disorders whom I have treated are some of the most intelligent, competent, creative, and hilarious people I have ever known. And they are anything but shallow in their reflections about themselves and the world around them.

Toward establishing a middle ground with humor on this subject, Jenni's lessons and stories contain humor that neither minimizes the struggle—hers, yours, or anyone else's—nor ridicules or condemns. The humor of *Life Without Ed* comes from Jenni's perspective from having been there—in the trenches. And that's what humor in personal growth work is anyway: perspective that is born of experience.

So I invite you to meet a remarkable young woman who will share with you secrets that many of you have thought—at least until now—were only your secrets.

I encourage you to take advantage of the short sections in *Life Without Ed*. Read a little from here and there throughout the book, in no particular order. Identify with what Jenni has to say to you, try some of the exercises, and make some notes in a journal of your own. But try not to put too much pressure on yourself. Take *Life Without Ed* a little at a time. Don't binge on it. Chew slowly and digest it in your own time frame. And certainly don't starve yourself of its wisdom.

Don't add this book to your list of compulsions. Read it, reread it, rest, and come back to it. When you are feeling particularly courageous, talk to a friend about what you are learning about yourself.

Enjoy. Grow. And be kind to yourself along the way.

— THOM RUTLEDGE

Introduction

I HAVE NEVER BEEN married, but I am happily divorced. Ed and I lived together for more than twenty years. He was abusive, controlling, and never once hesitated to tell me what he thought, how I was doing it wrong, and what I should be doing instead. I hated him, but I could not leave him. Ed convinced me that I needed him and that without him I was worthless, nothing special, and worse. He told me that he was looking out for my best interest—that his way was for my own good—but he always turned on me. He made promises that he never kept. When I hit bottom physically and emotionally, I finally decided to divorce him.

Let me tell you a little more about Ed. He is not a high school sweetheart. Ed is not some creep that I started dating in college. And Ed is not a guy that I met in the supermarket checkout line (although he does hang out a lot in grocery stores). Ed's name comes from the acronym E.D.—as in eating disorder. Ed is my eating disorder.

You might recognize Ed as the little voice inside that says, "You just need to lose a few more pounds," or, "Do you know how many calories are in that?" Ed is the one who stares back at you in the mirror and says that you should be dissatisfied with your appearance. Ed talks to all of us. While some of us are deeply embroiled in a relationship with him, others are just casually dating him. Maybe you are just meeting Ed for the first time. Whether you are married to Ed or just flirting with him, this book is for you.

I broke free from Ed, my eating disorder, through a therapeutic approach I learned from psychotherapist Thom Rutledge, which involves thinking of the eating disorder as a distinct being with unique thoughts and a personality separate from my own. In one of my first therapy sessions with Thom, he pulled up an extra chair and asked me to talk to the chair as if it were my eating disorder. Thom ignored the you-must-be-nuts look I gave him and continued, "If your eating disorder was sitting in this chair right now, what would you say to it?" Well, he was the professional; I was paying this man to help me, so I decided to give it a try. I looked at the chair and said, "Why do you try to control my every move? Why won't you just leave me alone?" In the few moments that it took me to ask those two questions, I felt a little separation from my eating disorder, and it felt so good. Throughout that therapy session, I continued this conversation with my eating disorder. By the end of the hour, I was referring to my eating disorder by a man's name, and for the first time, I had a feeling that I had just taken a significant step toward freedom.

Unlike the way I felt leaving sessions with previous therapists and psychiatrists, I left Thom's office that day with a solid sense of hope. Experiencing just a little bit of separation from Ed in Thom's session proved to me that I could succeed in recovery. I had never before felt this separation while working with other people. In fact, I often left their sessions feeling hopeless and more entrenched with my eating disorder. I would spend the entire therapy session crying and talking about how frustrated I was with recovery. I was never directed toward positive steps to help fight my eating disorder. Sure, some of these health care professionals offered advice, but it tended to be unrealistic and did not address the real issue of the eating disorder. For instance, one psychiatrist insisted that my problems would be solved if I went back to college and earned a second degree in music business. He was sure that this would help me change my behaviors with food. In reality, researching colleges and talking to admissions counselors served only to stress me out and distracted me from fighting my eating disorder head-on. So you can imagine my relief when Thom showed me a therapeutic approach that actually enabled me to speak directly to my eating disorder. It felt amazing to finally be able to tell my eating disorder exactly what I thought about it. For just a moment, I was able to experience Jenni—someone I had not seen in a long time.

Like many who use this approach, my eating disorder is male. Out of all of the people in my therapy group over the years, only one woman has referred to her eating disorder as female. She chose to call her eating disorder Edie. If your eating disorder is female, you might choose to replace "Ed" with "Edie" throughout this book. The important thing is to begin the separation.

I use the word *divorce* to describe my separation from Ed because of an analogy that I learned in therapy that compares a woman's relationship with her eating disorder to an abusive marriage in which the wife is controlled and even physically beaten. Similar to a battered wife who is scared to leave her husband, a woman with an eating disorder is afraid to leave her illness behind. Often, it is all she has ever known. Women in abusive marriages frequently hide their bruises from friends and family in the same way that women with eating disorders hide their battle scars. These wives will begin healing only when they take the first step of deciding to divorce their abusers. And that is the only way that women with eating disorders can taste that same freedom in life. If you have never been married, you can think of this separation from Ed as breaking up with a significant other or even severing ties with a best friend. Again, the important thing to remember is separation.

In therapy, I learned that recovery is not about eliminating the eating disorder but is about changing my relationship with it. The relationship I had with Ed completely changed through the course of our separation in the same way that the relationship that a married couple has transforms through the process of a divorce. In order to change my relationship with Ed, I had to learn to stand back and separate myself from him. I had to make room for my own opinion, which created the opportunity for me to disagree with Ed. I realized that my food obsessions and my condemnation of my own body were coming from Ed, not me. To this day, recovery is about making room for the real me to exist.

My first memories of Ed are from when I was only four years old. Ed would tease me in dance class and say that I was the largest girl in the room. He told me that my legs were fat because my thighs rubbed together in my leotard. When I was onstage, it did not matter whether or not I got the dance routine right. All that mattered was how thin I looked in my costume. I obsessed in elementary school when I was not allowed to stand in the front row in class photos—the row with the small, petite children. Ed explained, "You are in the middle row because you are fat. If you were skinny, you would be in the front row." Oddly enough, there is no photographic evidence that I was overweight. The pictures do prove that I was taller than those kids in the front row. But Ed never said that I was taller; he said plainly that I was fatter. Ed began restricting my food intake as a child by never letting me eat sweets—no Thanksgiving pie, no birthday cake, and no Halloween candy.

During high school, Ed always forbade me to eat lunch. In show choir rehearsal, he made me stare into the wall-to-wall mirrors and analyze who was the thinnest girl in the group. Ed told me that if I wanted to be a successful singer, I would have to be thinner. In college, he restricted my food drastically. Eventually, he began forcing me to eat huge amounts of food. In order to stay thin, he convinced me to purge, which meant throwing up, fasting, or overexercising. Ed loved this cycle of bingeing and purging. On a binge, it was not uncommon for me to drive from Taco Bell to McDonald's to Wendy's at 1:00 A.M. or even to eat cookies out of a trash can. Ed controlled my life.

Separating from Ed was not an easy task. Throughout my recovery, I learned to ask myself repeatedly, "Is that what I think or what Ed thinks?" My answer was usually "Ed." I always knew what Ed thought but had to really search to find out what was going on in Jenni's mind. Oddly, I realized that I knew Ed very well but frequently felt as if I had never even met Jenni.

Initially, I simply learned how to distinguish Ed's voice from mine. In the beginning I agreed 100 percent with whatever Ed said.

If he said I was fat, I agreed. If he said go to the store, I went. If he said eat until I tell you to stop, I did.

Slowly, I began to disagree with Ed, but even in disagreement I still obeyed his commands. In many ways, I felt weaker than ever. If Ed told me that I should not eat lunch, I knew that he was wrong, but I wouldn't eat lunch. Now, besides feeling weak, I felt like I was going crazy. I knew the right things to do but didn't do them. I never thought of myself as someone who could be easily controlled, but that is exactly what was going on.

As part of therapy, I kept a journal. I learned to write dialogue between Ed and me. To help you separate from your Ed, I will include dialogue throughout the book. Here is an example:

> **ED:** I can't believe that you are going to eat lunch today.
> **JENNI:** My friend is taking me out. I have no choice.
> **ED:** When it comes to ordering from the menu, I'm in charge.
> **JENNI:** (nodding head) Of course.
> **ED:** We'll just play with your food and hide it under napkins.
> **JENNI:** OK.

With persistence and an increasing determination fueled by my growing frustration, I finally began to disobey his commands. Here is another example of my dialogue with Ed:

> **ED:** Jenni, I know you feel horrible. That awful impending-doom feeling will go away if you just walk to the vending machine and eat as much as you possibly can.
> **JENNI:** That's not true. If I do what you say, I'll only end up feeling much worse.
> **ED:** You'll feel relief. You'll feel calm. If you just binge, that terrible feeling will disappear just like it always does.
> **JENNI:** If I listen to you, I will only feel a momentary numbness. Then I will feel guilty, ashamed, and angry, and I'll still feel awful.

ED: Stop trying to fight me. Just go to the snack machine and pick out some of your favorites.

JENNI: No. I think I'll pick up the phone instead and call someone for support who understands what I am going through. I don't need you anymore.

Writing out this dialogue, which can be so helpful in separating from Ed, has been included as one of Thom's therapeutic exercises, which you will find at the end of parts 1 through 6 of the book. Thom will make suggestions and share exercises that have been milestones in my recovery. I cannot guarantee that every activity in this book will help you, but I will say that each one was a significant step in my journey. Some of the exercises may seem silly at first, and Ed will tell you that they are all a waste of time. I encourage you to try even those exercises that seem ridiculous. *Life Without Ed* includes only a bare minimum of exercises—so minimal that there is hardly any caloric content. Do not feel as if you have to complete all of the activities. On a second pass through the book, you may learn a lot from an activity that you did not find helpful the first time through. Take what is helpful and leave the rest.

The format of this book is specifically designed for the individual who struggles with an eating disorder. When Ed and I were married, my thoughts were so consumed by food and weight that I found it hard to concentrate on anything else. Reading was especially challenging because of the difficulty in concentrating and the almost impossibility of my sitting still long enough to read. I often had to read the same page in a book over and over again. Taking into account the decreased concentration that you may experience, this book is divided into bite-sized, easily digestible portions. I have discovered that it is easier to stay focused on one short section as compared to a long chapter composed of page after page of text.

Another reason for short sections is to accommodate your busy schedule. I know that you are busy, because I know eating disorders are so time-consuming that there is little time left for anything else. If you are like me, you spend most of your time meeting Ed's demands. Short sections are beneficial in that they can be read quickly. In just moments, you will gain an amount of information that you can understand, remember, and apply to your life. And you can read a complete section before Ed has a chance to stop you.

In addition to short sections, you will find humor throughout this book. Just because you might laugh does not mean that the topic addressed is not deadly serious. We are going to have fun along this journey, but there is nothing funny about what Ed will do to you. Humor has been an important element in my recovery—helping me to break away from my belief that I would never recover and providing me with a new perspective on my eating disorder. The ability to laugh at Ed gave me a feeling of power that enabled me to take charge of my life.

Even though this book was designed especially for the person suffering with an eating disorder, Ed enjoys reading each and every page. Ed will read right along with you and try to make use of what he learns. Do you hear him now? As you read, listen for Ed's responses to the ideas within the book. Practice distinguishing Ed's responses from yours. You are not Ed. He will take from the book what he wants, but your job is to stay focused on what you need for your recovery—for your life.

This may seem strange, but I am not going to try to explain eating disorders. When I first entered into recovery, I made the mistake of believing that I could "think" my eating disorder away. I read every book on the subject. I fell back on my B.S. in biochemistry and my interest in medicine as I tried to understand exactly why I had an eating disorder, how it had developed, and what specific chemical signals were misfiring in my brain. I thought that if I understood everything, I could think my way out of it. I was wrong. It came to a point when I finally had to stare Ed in the face and take action. In this book, I share my experience, strength, and hope that finally broke the chains that bound me to Ed.

This book is about letting go, falling down and getting back up again, and realizing that you are not alone. The reality is that millions of people across the globe suffer from eating disorders. While most individuals with eating disorders are female, males also struggle. I am inclined to believe that we don't have an accurate count of the true number of males who battle the illness. Years ago, alcoholism was mistakenly thought to be a man's disease, as women were suffering in silence. Comparably, I believe that many men have not yet come forward about having an eating disorder. You will see a lot of references to females throughout this book, because my close-knit therapy group (which I mention frequently) has included all women, and, of course, I am a woman. But this book is beneficial to both men and women.

You may be anywhere on the continuum between thinking, "I don't have an eating disorder" to "I am enthusiastic about recovering from my eating disorder." Eating disorders are characterized by denial. When I was at my very worst, people confronted me daily about my weight and asked me if I had anorexia. I considered this to be the greatest compliment. You may feel at two different places on this continuum within the same day or even hour. You are likely to experience resistance and mixed feelings. Regardless, I ask that you approach this book as open-mindedly as possible.

Just because I have written about recovery does not mean that I am so far removed from my own eating disorder that I don't know what it feels like to have one. In fact, it is because I know exactly what it feels like that I wanted to write this book so badly. Eating disorders are about constant self-criticism, loss of self-esteem, and unrelenting perfectionism. I know what it feels like to be trapped inside all of these—completely surrounded by Ed.

I know what it is like to feel pressured to be thin. I am currently pursuing a career in the music business—an industry with a very high physical standard. I turned down an acceptance to medical school to take a shot at being a recording artist. After college, I left everyone and everything that I knew back home in Texas and struck out on my own to Nashville, Music City U.S.A., to follow my dream—a dream that told me I had to have a perfect body. I gave up the chance of being a doctor to pursue a path with no guarantees, and I ended up face-to-face with my eating disorder. In Nashville, I found that most of the successful female singers were extremely thin. Ed told me that I had to be thinner. To this day, I still struggle with the idea that performers are supposed to be thinner than everyone else in the world.

In my life, I have trusted Ed over and over again, always willing to give him another chance, only to discover that his solutions make me feel worse. I no longer trust him, and I have divorced him, but I do still have occasional slips. I am a work in progress—not perfect. I am grateful that I now understand perfection is not the goal.

I know what it is like to have an eating disorder, and I know what it takes to get through it. In this book, due to my attempts to keep each story short, it may seem to you that recovery has been simple for me. In my effort to be concise, it may seem that I frequently overcame Ed in a matter of moments. For instance, in the first paragraph of a story, I may be in the pits of hell. Then, by the third paragraph, everything is just wonderful, and life couldn't be better. I assure you that my struggles with Ed have never been that easy. Although the second paragraph in the story may not be very long on paper, it symbolizes lots of hard work, sweat and tears, anger mixed with depression, hopelessness, a fair amount of resistance, and probably days of dedication to recovery.

Separating from Ed was very challenging and seemed impossible at times. I just had to believe in myself and be willing to fall down over and over again. I had to find the strength to get back up—every time. And Thom can verify that I fell down repeatedly. Sometimes it took days to get back up again. But the important thing is that I did eventually get up every time. Words on paper cannot adequately describe what it is really like to overcome an eating disorder. One must experience it to truly understand.

No book or program is going to simply take away your eating disorder. To recover, you are going to have to eat, and you are going to have to stop bingeing and purging. And you are going to have to separate yourself from Ed and meet yourself all over again—or possibly for the first time. Recovery is about a new outlook on life. It is about little changes that lead to big changes. Changes that last take time. So do your best to practice patience.

Do not try to do it all by yourself. I tried that, and it didn't work. In order to move along the recovery path, you will need to surround yourself with supportive people. My support team includes family, friends, and the girls in my therapy group. It also includes my dietitian, Susan, and my internist, Dr. Tucker. And, of course, there is my psychotherapist, Thom. It took the help of all of these people for me to get to the amazing life that I enjoy today.

I have heard it said about some things that "From the outside looking in, you can't understand it. From the inside looking out, you can't explain it." This is a wonderful description of an eating disorder. People who do not have an eating disorder cannot possibly understand it. They are not expected to any more than those of us with eating disorders are able to explain it. In my recovery, my parents were able to truly provide support only when we all accepted that they would never understand what Ed drives me to think and do. They often say, "I don't understand, but I support you." People don't have to understand us. We just need them to believe us. If I tell my mom that I "feel fat," I do not need her to convince me that I am not fat. Instead, I just need her to believe that I really do feel fat. She does not understand what that feels like, but she believes me. That's what I need.

Sometimes in recovery, it is difficult to see exactly where you are headed. This new way of life seems to take you on a path where the destination is unclear. As Dr. Tucker says, "Direction is important, not destination." Focus on the right path. If you stay pointed in the right direction, you do not have to worry about arriving at the proper place. By choosing to read this book, you are journeying in the right direction. Don't worry if you make some wrong turns along the way. I have learned that each wrong turn is a valuable lesson as long as I keep walking.

And as long as you keep walking, you will be on your way to happiness, serenity, and divorce (from Ed, of course). For this divorce, you won't need an expensive attorney, a judge, or even a spouse. As I said in the beginning, I have never been married. No, you don't need a ring on your finger to divorce Ed. All you need is the willingness to keep turning the pages in this book, in your recovery, and in your life. And when you come across that page that looks like a divorce decree, you will be ready to pick up a pen, sign your name, and make it final. You will be free.

Update for the Tenth Anniversary Edition

Even though you just read a couple of pages back that I "still have occasional slips," I'm excited to say—ten years later—that is no longer the case. I am freer than I ever thought possible when I originally wrote this book. That is why I included an afterword in this anniversary edition. You will also find specific sections for males, loved ones, and professionals as well as an actual divorce decree to sign. What you won't see are significant edits to the original content of *Life Without Ed*. While perfectionism initially suggested changing everything from titles to deleting entire sections, I decided to stay true to my reality at the time of writing the book. To take advantage of today's technology, however, I added some new ideas, which you will see included as brief notes at the bottom of select pages. (A decade ago, phones were used simply for making calls!) So what you hold in your hands is the experience of a twenty-something navigating early recovery combined with the insights of a woman who is fully recovered. If I had seen those last two words—*fully recovered*—next to one another in the original manuscript for *Life Without Ed*, I would have called it a typo. Now, I am grateful to call it my life. You can find this freedom, too. As I said earlier (and more than ten years ago), just keep walking.

"You must do the thing you think you cannot do."

—Eleanor Roosevelt

1

FILING FOR DIVORCE

Separating from Ed

The first step in breaking free from Ed was learning how to distinguish between the two of us. I had to determine which thoughts came from Ed and which ones belonged to me. Next I had to learn to disagree with and disobey Ed. This was not easy. This took time, lots of patience, and a willingness to keep trying over and over again. Part 1 will help you begin to look at the differences between Ed and yourself. Practice separating from him, and you will be taking your first steps toward divorce.

Declaration of Independence

BINGEING, PURGING, AND STARVING. Why couldn't I stop bingeing, purging, and starving? Why couldn't I just eat like "normal" people do? Because Ed was in control. I tried daily to win battles against him. I tried daily, and I lost daily. No matter how much effort I put forward, I still found myself in the same patterns of bingeing, purging, and starving. I made promises to myself forbidding these behaviors only to break them before the end of the day—sometimes before the end of the hour.

Although I had finally realized that I could not have the life that I wanted with Ed, at the same time, I could not imagine my life without him. So for years I told myself that I would change things, but in the back of my mind, I always knew that I would be with Ed. It was inevitable. I hated Ed and wanted to be free of him, but there was still a small part of me that would not let him go.

As I learned more about Ed's plans for my life and more about myself, I grew angrier about his lies. Ed told me that the beauty of a woman was in the figure that she carries and the number that appears when she steps on a scale. Ed said that Marilyn Monroe, once considered the icon of American beauty, was fat, because she was larger than today's rail-thin models. According to Ed, I needed to look like the Barbie doll that I used to play with as a child. I have heard it said that if Barbie were a real woman, she would have to walk on all fours due to her proportions. (She's so impossibly top-heavy, not to mention tiny-waisted, that she would topple over.) Ed wanted me to conform to unrealistic standards.

If I could just keep my weight low enough, Ed said that I could be in complete control of my life. If I was small enough, I could fit myself into any box deemed appropriate for any situation. If I did not take up too much space, I would not get in anyone's way. Everyone would like me. And, of course, Ed told me that he made me special and that without him, I was nothing. If I just stayed with him, he would make me perfect in every way.

After living with the reality of Ed's lies for long enough, after becoming extremely frustrated and depressed, and after hitting rock bottom, I finally wanted to let go of Ed forever. I wanted to make a wholehearted commitment to separate from him, so I wrote my declaration of independence from Ed. I modeled my declaration after the United States Declaration of Independence, and surprisingly, I found that I did not have to change too many words. It seems that in those days England was just as big of a tyrant to the American colonies as Ed is to me today. I read my declaration of independence out loud to my therapy group, and they signed it for me to show their support. My declaration of independence marked the first time in my recovery that I made a solid commitment to break free from Ed. After making my declaration, I still struggled daily, but I was committed to getting back up and staying true to my words.

Today my declaration of independence hangs on the wall of my bedroom with the signatures of delegates from my group.

My Declaration of Independence

When in the course of human events, it becomes necessary for one woman, Jenni, to dissolve the bonds which have connected her to Ed, and to assume, among the powers of the earth, the separate and equal station to which the Laws of Nature and Nature's God entitle her, a decent respect to the opinions of mankind requires that she should declare the causes which impel her to the separation.

We hold these truths to be self-evident, that all mankind are endowed by their Creator with certain unalienable Rights, that among these are Life, Liberty, and the pursuit of happi-

ness. That whenever Ed becomes destructive of these ends, it is right to abolish Ed and to institute Recovery, laying its foundation on such principles and in such form as shall seem the most likely to effect safety and happiness. When a long train of abuses, pursuing invariably the same woman evinces a design to reduce her under absolute despotism, it is her right, it is her duty, to throw off Ed, and to provide Recovery for her future security. The history of Ed is a history of repeated injuries, all having in direct object the establishment of an absolute Tyranny over Jenni. To prove this, let facts be submitted.

- *Ed has refused for a long time, for Jenni to find happiness.*
- *Ed has erected a multitude of binges and purges.*
- *Ed has ravaged Jenni's life and harmed the lives of people close to her.*
- *Ed has joined with Perfectionism to subject Jenni to acts foreign to her constitution.*
- *Ed has excited domestic insurrections within Jenni.*
- *Ed has cut off emotions.*
- *Ed has suspended Jenni's own mind and declared himself invested with the power to legislate Jenni's world.*
- *Ed has deprived Jenni of food.*
- *Ed has taken away Jenni's feelings, abolished her most valuable morals, and altered fundamentally her values.*

In every stage of these oppressions, Jenni has petitioned for Redress in the most humble terms. Her repeated Petitions have been answered only by repeated injury. Jenni must, therefore, acquiesce in the necessity, which denounces her Separation, and hold Ed as the Enemy.

Jenni, therefore, solemnly publishes and declares that she is Free and Independent; that she is absolved from all alle-

giance to Ed, that all connection between Ed and her ought to be totally dissolved, and that as a free and independent woman she has the full power to eat, live in peace, and to do all other acts and things which independent people do. And for the support of the Declaration, with a firm reliance on the Protection of Divine Providence, Jenni mutually pledges to her therapy group her life, fortune, and sacred honor.

Beth Julia Lisa Mary Julie Nikki
Heather Laura Jennie Melissa Morgan
Kristina Jen Stephanie Stephanie Nikki

After I wrote my declaration of independence and shared it with others, I was committed to not turning back. I devoted myself entirely to moving forward and divorcing Ed. I knew that I would be traveling a long and difficult road—the hardest one I had ever walked (and even crawled at some points)—but I also knew that it would be worth it. And it has been.

Downloadable "Declaration of Independence from Ed" available at jennischaefer .com/independence.

Making the Split

E D WAS REALLY depressed in group therapy one night. Julie talked about walking out on Ed at the movie theater on Saturday. Lisa finally agreed not to let Ed in the next time he knocked on her door, and Kelly made a commitment to not let Ed drive her home from group anymore. Everyone was making progress in the struggle to separate from Ed—with the exception of Eileen, a shy, first-time group member. At the end of the session, with a confused expression on her face, she looked around at all of us and asked, "Who's Ed?"

No one had explained to Eileen that Ed was each of our individual eating disorders. Throughout the entire ninety-minute session, she had imagined that Ed was some creep that we were all dating. I often forget how strange the concept of Ed seems to newcomers. The truth is that it has not always been easy for me to separate from Ed. After all, for more than twenty years, Ed and I had been one and the same.

I remember the first time that I made the split with Ed in group. I was speaking about how horrible my week had been and began to cry. Instead of offering me a tissue to wipe away my tears, Thom handed me an authentic Darth Vader mask and actually asked me to put it on. I had no idea where he was going with this, but I had seen stranger things in group, so I put on the mask. With my entire head covered by the black plastic, Thom asked me to pretend to be Ed. Specifically, he asked me to play the role of Ed and speak directly to Jenni. This was a piece of cake (pun intended). The comments that arose were the same ones that I had heard all week long: "Jenni, you are fat. You will never recover. You will be miserable for the rest of your life." Next, I took the mask off and played the role of Jenni—separate from Ed. This was difficult. After encouragement from the group, I finally said, "Ed, you are a liar. You are manipulative, and I will get away from you." Through this role-play, I began to see, hear, and feel the difference between Ed and me.

From that moment on, whenever I spoke in group, someone would ask, "Who is talking now? Is it Ed or Jenni?" I began to realize how frequently Ed expressed his opinion through my mouth. Sometimes we would pull out the Darth Vader mask in order to help me make the split. Today, I do not need Darth Vader to distinguish myself from Ed. In fact, the mask is shoved to the back of a shelf in the group therapy room, and Ed is no longer front and center in my life.

Disagree and Disobey

W**HEN** I **FIRST** began recovery, a typical conversation between Ed and me went something like this:

ED: You should not eat dinner.
JENNI: I know. I won't eat dinner.

I agreed with what Ed said, and I obeyed him. After many solid months of recovery, our conversation became:

ED: You should not eat dinner.
JENNI: You are wrong. I should eat dinner, but I just can't.

Even though I disagreed with Ed, I still obeyed him. Today, when Ed and I talk, it looks more like this:

ED: You should not eat dinner.
JENNI: You are wrong. I should eat dinner, and I will.

The ultimate goal is to disagree with and disobey Ed.

As you practice separating from Ed, you will begin to make room for your own opinion—creating an opportunity for you to disagree with Ed. The thought of disagreeing may seem very scary and unrealistic to you. These responses are natural and understandable considering the power Ed has had over your life. But as you continue to see yourself as separate from Ed, you will slowly learn to distinguish between what he is telling you and what you really think. You will realize that Ed—not you—is the one who thinks you should binge and purge. You will find the part of yourself that wants to abandon those behaviors and be healthy. Ed wants you to binge and purge; you want to live.

Don't worry if you cannot disagree with Ed immediately. It took me many months to be able to disagree with him. I had to look closely at what I wanted for my life and compare that to Ed's goals before I realized that I did, in fact, disagree with his ideas. I had to practice acknowledging this disagreement over and over again, and I slowly learned to voice my own opinion. Although it takes time and patience, you, too, will be able to disagree with those habitual negative thoughts that follow you around night and day.

After you become comfortable disagreeing with Ed, the next step is to disobey him. I found disobeying Ed even more—a lot more—difficult than disagreeing with him. After I began to disagree with what Ed would tell me, I continued to follow his orders. I still binged, purged, and starved. If Ed told me not to eat dinner, I knew that he was wrong. I knew that everyone on my support team would want me to eat dinner, but I still just could not do it. I could not break the behaviors. But, as I continued to disagree with Ed, I learned more about myself and became stronger. I gained a greater sense of independence from my eating disorder. One step at a time, I was able to disobey Ed's commands.

Previously, I said that the ultimate goal is to disagree with and disobey Ed. Because we do not live in a perfect world, sometimes this ultimate goal is not attainable. Although it would be wonderful if we could always disagree with and disobey Ed, that is not the only way that we can be successful in recovery. We are also practicing good recovery if we agree with Ed but still disobey him. For instance, sometimes, even today, this is the conversation we have:

ED: You are fat. Don't eat today.
JENNI: You are right. I feel fat today, but I am still going to eat today.

Sometimes when Ed tells me I am fat, I agree with him, but I am still making progress in recovery when I choose to disobey him. While it is possible to agree with Ed and be in recovery, obeying him is never an option.

When Ed talks to you, always try to separate from him, disagree with what he is saying, and disobey him. Sometimes the best that you will be able to do is to just disobey him. That means that you are not perfect. But it also means that you are still making progress along your journey to freedom. You will get there.

Ed's Rules

I STEPPED ON THE elevator with three other people. That made a total of five of us on that elevator. Yes, I did say five. Ed was also along for the ride. As soon as the elevator doors shut and we headed up, Ed whispered in my ear, "Congratulations, Jenni. You are the thinnest person on this elevator. You are really special today." The elevator stopped at floor three, and a very petite woman stepped inside.

Ed immediately said, "Jenni, that woman is thinner than you. You are so large. You have really let yourself go." From the ground floor to level three, I felt as if I had gained twenty or thirty pounds. Have you ever gained weight while riding an elevator? If you have, then you must be familiar with one of Ed's favorite rules: "You must always be the thinnest person in any given place at any given time."

Ed has rules for everything. There are the wardrobe rules: "Your 'skinny' jeans must always fit your body loosely," and, "On the days that you binge, you must wear your baggy clothes." Then, there is the dining rule: "You must always eat less than the people you are dining with on any occasion." Your Ed may have slightly different rules for you, but one thing is for sure. He has rules, and he expects you to follow them.

What happens if you do not follow Ed's rules? When I don't obey Ed, he tells me that I am a worthless individual. He says, "If you don't do what I am saying, you will never be successful. People will just look down on you for your whole life. You will never realize your full potential."

On the other hand, if I listen to Ed and do what he says, he tells me, "You are so special. You are doing what 'normal' people can't do. You are a success. If you keep listening to me, your life will be wonderful. You will always be in control." In reality, you must remember who is really in control—Ed.

When you are trying to begin your separation from Ed, it is important that you first recognize Ed's rules in your life. You must be able to distinguish between standards that Ed holds for you and healthy boundaries that you set for yourself. You must realize that Ed's rules do not make sense. For instance, many of Ed's rules contradict each other. On one day, Ed tells you not to touch that ice cream or dare drink that soda. Then, the very next day, Ed says, "Eat that entire gallon of ice cream, and drink three cans of soda. Eat as much as you can until you feel sick." Ed's rules are designed to harm us.

After you are able to recognize Ed's rules in your life, you must try to disagree with and disobey them. Even if it seems impossible for you to actually disagree with one of Ed's rules, you must still try to disobey him. If you are able to break his rules no matter what, you are taking a huge step toward separating from Ed. Disobeying Ed means you are moving in the right direction. Don't expect it to be easy.

Ed still has his same old rules for me, but I do not have to follow them anymore. Today I act from a position of personal strength and positive self-esteem. I order what I really want to eat in a restaurant. I wear clothes that are comfortable and that I feel good in. And I can even ride up an elevator without going up a dress size.

Ms. Perfectionist

ALTHOUGH I SEE Thom for "individual" therapy, there is a whole group of us in his office for each of my sessions. In fact, every place to sit in his office is occupied. Ed is sprawled out on the couch, while Thom and I sit in two cushioned chairs. And in the straight-back wooden chair sits Ms. Perfectionist, with perfect posture.

You see, Ed has many colleagues. Thom refers to one as the Should Monster, who tells me everything I should or should not have done in my life. I frequently hear the Timekeeper, who keeps a close eye on how I spend every minute of my day—making sure that each moment is spent productively. And I hear Ms. Perfectionist compromising to stay in line with the Timekeeper, promising she will make me perfect.

Nothing is ever good enough for Ms. Perfectionist. She is the one who insisted that I maintain a 4.00 grade point average in college. She wants everyone to like me, and she urges me to never make a mistake. I have realized that Ms. Perfectionist's constant striving for the impossible does not make me any better of a person. Instead, it just tears me down. In the same way that I separated from Ed, I have learned how to break away from Ms. Perfectionist.

In therapy, I began to distinguish my voice from hers. By separating from Ms. Perfectionist, I learned how to ease up on myself. I came to understand that it is Ms. Perfectionist—not me—who wants me to be perfect. When I still struggle with aspects of perfectionism, I acknowledge her and have a conversation with her. In the beginning, our conversations looked something like this:

Ms. Perfectionist: Jenni, you can't go to that party tonight.

Jenni: Why not? All of my friends will be there, and I really want to go.

Ms. Perfectionist: You can't go, because you binged today. You were not perfect today, and you don't deserve to go. And besides, you look too fat.

Jenni: You're right. I don't deserve to go, and I am fat.

At first, all I could do was separate from Ms. Perfectionist. I could distinguish between her voice and mine, but I still agreed with her and did what she wanted me to do. Today our dialogue sounds more like this:

Ms. Perfectionist: Jenni, you can't go to that party tonight.

Jenni: I am going to the party. All of my friends will be there, and I really want to go.

Ms. Perfectionist: You can't go, because you binged today. You were not perfect today, and you don't deserve to go. And besides you look too fat.

Jenni: I did binge today, but that doesn't mean I need to deprive myself of fun tonight. And I'm not fat.

It took many dialogues with Ms. Perfectionist (as it did with Ed) to get to the point where I could not only separate from her but also take a stand against her and for myself.

When I am talking to Thom in sessions these days, Ms. Perfectionist still likes to throw her two cents worth in every once in a while. If Thom says that I am doing well, she says that I should be doing better. If I am excited about some recent triumph in my recovery, she says that I should have done it sooner. I am definitely not perfect. But I learned in therapy that I do not have to be.

All I have to be is persistent. Each day I have to keep putting one foot down in front of the other. Slowly, I am replacing perfectionism with persistence. After all, in recovery and life it is persistence that really pays off. Forget about perfection.

Enlist Support

I F YOU WERE battling cancer, would you try to do it alone? Would you refuse to see a doctor, convinced that you could save yourself? Would you hide your disease from friends and family, refusing to receive their support? Of course not. You would enlist the support of those around you to help fight a life-threatening illness.

Your eating disorder is a life-threatening illness. Do you have a support team? If your answer is yes, that is great! Keep reaching out. There is no such thing as too much support.

If you do not have the support that you need yet, you probably feel the way I did when I first realized that I had an eating disorder. I really did not want to be a burden to those around me. I was also ashamed, embarrassed, and afraid. I did not want anyone to know that I was not perfect. I thought that I was weak if I could not solve my "little" problem on my own. After all, I had done everything else in my life on my own. Why should this be any different?

So I went to the bookstore and bought every book that I could find on eating disorders. I did research on the Internet and learned all kinds of interesting facts and statistics. I was sure that I could save myself.

I was wrong. I did not even come close to changing my eating disorder behaviors on my own. It was so difficult trying to divorce Ed without having anyone to talk to about my struggles. I kept everything inside until I reached a point where I thought I was going to crumble. I could see my life falling apart before my eyes. The more I tried to fight Ed alone, the more he took hold of me. I finally decided to tell someone. I had to risk feeling ashamed and embarrassed. I had to risk losing my image of being perfect. And I had to risk being considered a burden to others. My only other option was to continue down the path with Ed, a path that predictably leads to destruction and even death.

When I finally decided to tell David, my boyfriend at the time, about my struggles with food, I found that I literally could not speak. I was crying hysterically, but I could not say a word. I could not even look him in the eye. I felt so ashamed. So I hid a brochure on eating disorders under a pillow in my living room. I left the room, ducked under the covers in my bed, and told David to look under the pillow on the couch. That's how I told him, because I could not say anything.

The next people I wanted to talk to were my parents. Once again, I found myself in a situation where I could not speak. So David spoke to my parents for me, while I cried by his side. After talking to David and my parents, I decided that I needed to get professional help. Searching for eating disorder specialists and finding someone covered by my insurance plan was a tedious task. Despite the tremendous effort required, I highly encourage you to seek help from qualified health care professionals.

Now I have a very large support team. I would not have made it this far without them. They stood behind me when I first confronted Ed. They gave me words of hope and encouragement when I needed them. They helped me up when I fell down. (They still do that today.) And I was surprised to find out that no one considers me to be a burden. In fact, when people offer me support, they say that it makes them feel really good about themselves. I also got over my feelings of shame. No one treated me as if I had any reason to feel badly about myself. The people on my support team actually said that they admired me more than ever for reaching out for help. They said I was an inspiration; they were proud of me.

You do not have to face Ed alone. If you are afraid to reach out, build your support team slowly. Tell just one friend about your eating disorder. Feel the support that you get from that one person. And imagine what it would feel like with more people on your side. Begin to seek help from other trusted individuals. Make an appointment with a therapist or dietitian who works with eating disorders. Do it according to your time frame, but build a support team. None of us can do it alone.

To begin enlisting support, see Resources in the back of this book. Connect with others in recovery and find treatment professionals in your area. You can even chat online with a trained volunteer at the National Eating Disorders Association.

Not Just Anyone

I DIDN'T CHOOSE JUST anyone to be on my eating disorder support team. No, I didn't want just anyone to play such a vital role in my recovery. Whom did I choose? First I chose a friend who was completely lost in his own alcoholism. He could not take care of himself, but I was sure that he could support me on my road back to health. Then I chose another guy with whom I had only had a few dates and who cared more about hockey than he did about me. Finally, I chose a friend who was 100 percent devoted to my getting better as long as I did everything (and I do mean everything) her way.

First, let me tell you about the not-interested-in-recovery alcoholic, Michael. Late one night I relapsed and was feeling very low. I showed up on Michael's doorstep. I could see that he had been drinking as soon as he opened the door.

I sat down on his couch and said, "I feel horrible. I just relapsed. I don't think I can do it. I don't think I will ever put my eating disorder behind me."

He replied, "You don't have an eating disorder. You don't have any problems at all. People starving in Africa have problems."

I answered, "Well, I certainly feel like I have problems. And I do have an eating disorder. You should see what I do with food."

"Whatever," he said, "It's simple. You just need to eat three meals a day. No big deal. You don't know what real problems are."

I was not in the mood to convince my friend that I had an eating disorder and to prove that such an illness really is life-threatening, so I left. I walked to my car, sat down, and cried with my head over the steering wheel. I'm sure that he just kept drinking.

Then there is Jesse, the guy I was dating who cared more about hockey than about anything else. Late one night, I was really frustrated with recovery, so I picked up the phone and called him.

"I'm feeling really hopeless right now," I said, "I just don't know if I have the strength to keep fighting my eating disorder."

"Guess what? We won our hockey game tonight. I scored three goals. It was my best game ever," he said.

I asked, "Did you even hear what I said?"

"You should have seen my first goal," he answered. "The crowd went wild. It was so cool."

I quickly said good-bye, hung up the phone, and went to the refrigerator to binge.

Finally, there is Denise—my friend who knew exactly what I needed to do in order to recover. We went out to lunch one day. I ordered a meal that satisfied all of my food plan requirements.

Denise quickly said, "I don't think you should have ordered that. The grilled chicken sandwich looks like something that would be better for you. You're never going to succeed at recovery if you don't start doing some things right."

"But Denise," I said, "My dietitian said that what I ordered is a perfectly good meal for me."

"Who's your dietitian? I am not sure that she knows what she is talking about. I really think you should listen to me," she replied.

Denise made it quite clear throughout the meal that she was unhappy with my meal selection and that I should have listened to her.

As you can see, calling these three people a "support" team is a bit of a stretch. Luckily, at the time, I did have some truly helpful individuals on my support team. They were Thom, Susan, and Dr. Tucker.

I went to Thom's office and told him about the difficulty I was having with finding people to support me outside of the health care profession. I described Michael, Jesse, and Denise.

"Jenni," Thom said, "You need to be more careful; choose wisely. There are certain things that you need to look for in people who can really support you."

Thom continued to talk about the qualities that I should look for in people who were going to be on my support team. These people had to genuinely care about me as a person. They had to be empathetic and good listeners. They needed to realize that they did not need to tell me what to do in recovery but instead should work with me to reach goals that I set for myself. These people needed to be flexible and realize that recovery is a one-day-at-a-time process. I had to feel comfortable turning to these people when I was at my very worst. And these people had to be willing to lend me a hand when I was down.

I left the session with Thom and really thought about who I would recruit for my new and improved support team. Obvious choices were the girls in my therapy group. I chose Emily, who had invited me to my first group therapy session, and I included members of my family. I told my family that I didn't need for them to understand what I was going through; that I just needed them to listen to me, believe me, and love me. I asked my friends if there were times when they preferred I not call, so I would know whom I could call on in the middle of the night. And I decided to be in touch with people from my support team every single day.

I have seen that a great support team makes all of the difference in recovery. I would not be where I am today without the people on whom I depend for support.

When you decide who will be on your support team, think of the qualities that you will need in a person when you are feeling discouraged. Think of people in your life who really care about you and who are interested in your recovery. Not just anyone can be depended upon for support. Not just anyone can hold your hand as you make the most difficult journey of your life. Not just anyone.

Ed's Other Brides

WHAT WAS THOM talking about? He kept mentioning divorce, and I wasn't even married. (I was wondering which one of us really needed therapy.) The idea of thinking of my eating disorder—if that is what it was—as a guy named Ed seemed ridiculous. Thom kept saying, "Separate from Ed," and, "Divorce Ed." He can be so redundant. How could I separate from someone who didn't exist?

When I began recovery, I denied my ties to Ed. I knew that things were not going well in my life, and I realized that I had strange behaviors when it came to food. But I just could not believe that I had a serious problem. I knew that I had decided on my own to see a doctor who specializes in eating disorders, a therapist who has treated eating disorders for more than fifteen years, and a dietitian whose main clientele suffered with eating disorders. And I was attending a therapy group for women who struggled with the illness. But I was not sure why I was doing all of this. I thought to myself, "Why am I spending all of this money and time in therapy? I don't really have a problem." I would ask each health care professional over and over, "Do you really think I have an eating disorder?" They all nodded their heads, "Yes." But I wasn't convinced. After all, my behaviors with food were all so normal—to me. It was how I had always been. And I definitely did not think that I was thin enough to have an eating disorder.

I read book after book on the subject of eating disorders. In the first few pages, the authors often listed the diagnostic criteria for eating disorders. Somehow, I always used this list to disqualify myself. The criteria specified a certain number of times someone with bulimia binges per week. I didn't think I binged enough. The criteria also included how thin you had to be in order to have anorexia. Again, I did not think I was thin enough.

So I found myself in this strange new world surrounded by people who were telling me to divorce some guy that I didn't even know. No one could make me believe that I had an eating disorder, but my support team did convince me to stay in recovery. Thom would say to me, "OK. Let's just assume that you don't have an eating disorder. Now, what is the worst thing that could happen to you from all of this therapy?" Of course, the answer was that even if I didn't have an eating disorder, I was learning how to take care of myself. I was learning about myself and getting healthier. This convinced me to stay in recovery for an illness that I wasn't even sure that I had.

I cannot say exactly when it happened—the first time that I recognized Ed—the first time that I looked directly at his face and knew that those eyes had tormented me since I was four years old. I don't know the first time that I realized that I was not a single woman after all. It was a gradual process.

Today, as I sit in a circle in group therapy, I see Ed's other brides. They claim that they don't even know the guy. But the image is vivid. Ed is sitting right beside each of them—holding their hands. Or sometimes, someone is actually sitting on Ed's lap. Ed even carries some individuals in and out of the therapy room. I can see it, but I don't try to convince them. I know that sooner or later they will feel Ed's breath on their neck. And they will catch a glimpse of him in the mirror one day. The next thing you know, Ed's other brides will see the ring on their finger. But not now. Today, Ed's other brides are single women—wondering why they are sitting in a room with a bunch of girls who have eating disorders—just like I used to be.

True Value System

FOR ONE ENTIRE week, I was eating right and going to all of my therapy sessions, and I felt great. Then, Ed jumped on my back and convinced me to binge and purge—and not tell anyone about it.

Ed said, "You must lie to your therapy group tomorrow night and tell them that you are doing well." And Ms. Perfectionist chimed in, "Then, they won't think that you're a failure."

Ed continued, "And because I won't be letting you eat tomorrow, you won't be able to have lunch with your friend Melody. So just make up any old excuse and cancel with her. You will also need to lie to your mom when she calls and asks you how you are doing. Just say that you are doing absolutely fine and that nothing could be better."

Ed wanted me to lie to everyone who is closest to me.

Then, I remembered what I had learned in therapy about comparing my value system in life to Ed's value system. I realized that Ed and Jenni live by two completely different value systems. According to Ed, lying to friends and family is perfectly OK. I, on the other hand, do not feel comfortable being so dishonest. Sure, in the past I have done exactly what Ed told me to do and lied to anyone and everyone in order to cover up for him. But today I know that lying goes against what I believe in.

So, although Ed wanted me to lie about my recent relapse, I decided to live in congruence with my own value system. I told everyone the truth about what was going on with me. By being honest, I gained the support that I needed to get back on track.

Lying is only one of the differences between Ed's value system and my own. Another thing that sets us apart is that Ed values thinness above all else. Ed thinks that my size and shape are more important than who I am on the inside. He says that my self-worth is determined by whether or not I can fit into a particular pair of jeans. If I look deep inside myself, I know that being thin is not more important than everything else. I do not judge others by what they look like, and I know that I should not judge myself by my appearance either. When I am living according to my value system, I cherish who I am as a person, not as a number on the scale.

Ed's value system also allows me to be irritable and rude to anyone who gets in his way. When I am under Ed's influence, I say things that I normally would not say. Once I screamed at Susan, my dietitian, "I hate you!" She was getting in the way of Ed's plan for my life, so he encouraged me to yell and say something that I really didn't mean. My value system would not have me yelling at my dietitian, because I was taught to treat others with dignity and respect.

When I first learned to separate Ed's value system from my own, I was amazed at how often I went Ed's way. I would lie, cheat, and even steal if Ed wanted me to. It made me really angry to see how much influence—no, control—Ed had over my life. I felt ashamed that I had listened to him so many times. I had done some horrible things. But I realized that I did not need to wallow in shame, because my value system, which is what I really believe in, was still intact and strong. I just needed to make a greater effort to connect to it in my daily life—especially when Ed was around.

After much practice and frustration, I have learned how to stay focused on my true values in life, and I am more at peace with myself, because I am not living a contradiction. I look in the mirror today, and I am happy to see the person looking back at me. It is no longer Ed. It is me.

Whatever It Takes

IN THE BEGINNING, when Ed knocked on my door, I opened it wide for him to come on in. He always promised that he would stay just a little while. But, it was never that way. I did not tell Ed to leave, so he would stay as long as he wanted and then walk out the door leaving my home in a wreck and me feeling worn out, depressed, and hopeless. I would vow to never let him in again. The next time he knocked, I would always think, "This time will be different." But it never was.

Finally, with the help of therapy, I stopped inviting Ed into my life with open arms. At first, I began to be more cautious. When Ed knocked on the door, I would still answer, but I would just barely crack the door open. I quickly realized that if I opened the door even slightly, he would push it completely open and stomp his way into my world.

So eventually I stopped opening the door altogether. In fact, I now have four heavy-duty Ed-resistant locks on the one door to my home. After the door was no longer an option, Ed starting lurking around my windows. He would try to reach me by sneaking in through each window. And one by one, I had my landlord install extra locks on all of my windows. My home is now Ed-proof.

Do you think Ed left me alone at this point? No way. He decided to reach me by phone. So rather than answering my calls immediately, I began paying more attention. When Ed gave me a ring, instead of the screen displaying "Ed," he somehow disguised himself as "D. Pression," "I. M. Pain," or "Ms. Ery." But I always knew it was Ed and would not pick up the phone.

What did Ed do next? He got an e-mail account, of course. At first, I easily recognized his e-mails as ed@loser.com. Then, he changed his e-mail address and I began to notice his messages by the subject lines: "Miss Me?" "Reminder: You're Fat," and "Lose Ten Pounds in Ten Days." I finally got a great filter that removes junk mail from my mailbox. That easily took care of that. I just hope Ed doesn't find some other way to get his messages through to me online.

But Ed does not give up easily, and it just may come to that. If it does, I will take the necessary steps to keep Ed out of my life once again. I am willing to do whatever it takes to keep Ed at bay. Because I am willing to go to any lengths to remain separate from Ed, I am doing well in recovery. The minute that I let my guard down and stop being proactive is the moment that Ed will make his way back into my life.

I don't know how Ed will try to sneak into your life after you have shut the door on him. He may try the windows or even the chimney. He might start visiting you via the postal carrier. If you get a letter from Ed, treat it just as if it contains anthrax or some other biochemical weapon. Because Ed is just as hazardous to your health. Do whatever it takes to separate and maintain that separation from Ed.

If you have to, get a restraining order against him. After all, the police are used to dealing with low-life offenders like Ed. Maybe they will even give him some jail time. But even then, you must be cautious. Whose number do you think Ed will dial with his one allotted phone call?

Thom's Turn

1. Declaration of Independence

Jenni's declaration of independence marked a turning point in her recovery. After everyone in the group signed the declaration, she did not automatically stop bingeing, purging, and starving, but from that point on she never lost sight of her goal—to live a fulfilling life without Ed.

Write your own declaration of independence from Ed. Use Jenni's idea of following the actual Declaration of Independence as your model, or choose a different approach. *How* you write it is not nearly as important as *that* you write it.

Share your new document with your support team. Ask them to sign it along with you. You will need all of their support and words of encouragement because this declaration is just the beginning. It is the beginning of hard work that will yield a wonderful result: your separation from Ed.

2. Conversation with Ed

For this exercise, you will need two chairs. Face the chairs toward each other with about three feet in between them. Designate one chair as Ed's and one chair as yours. When you are sitting in Ed's chair, speak as if you are Ed. In that chair be only Ed. In your chair, practice being you—separate from the eating disorder. This is usually difficult at first. My clients often don't know much about who they are beyond Ed. But I promise that with practice, your voice will become stronger.

Begin a conversation from either chair, and be sure to remember which chair you are in. For instance, if you are sitting in your chair and Ed is mentally interrupting you, switch chairs and speak the interruption aloud. This may seem strange or even crazy at first, but the truth is we all talk to ourselves. We just need to get better at it.

Continue switching back and forth between chairs until you are positive that you have experienced yourself as separate from Ed. Practice this role-play at different times over the next week. Try the exercise when you feel really lost in your eating disorder, and try it again when you are having a good day. Mastery of this exercise will provide you with a clear awareness of where you stop and your eating disorder begins. Here is an example of a possible conversation between you and Ed:

> ED: Why are you doing this stupid exercise anyway? You don't need help with anything.
> YOU: I just don't want to feel this way anymore.
> ED: Then quit reading that silly book and just listen to me. With me, you are special. Without me, you are worthless.
> YOU: (No response; sitting in your chair silently.)
> ED: That's right. Quit trying to fight me. I'll take care of you.
> YOU: I may not be strong enough to fight you now, but one day I will be.

3. What to Do Today

Practice separation from Ed by writing the answers to the following questions in your journal every day for a week:

- What does Ed want me to do today?
- What do I need to do today to be in recovery?

This is simple but far from easy. Like anything worth learning, it takes dedicated practice. Stick with it. Learning to distinguish between Ed's voice and your genuine voice will be the foundation for your recovery.

To help you in remembering to answer the questions in exercise 3, set up alerts on your smartphone. Use built-in reminders, or try one of the many free "reminder" mobile apps available. The Rise Up eating disorder recovery app will allow you to create custom alert messages, too. In addition to setting up reminders, you can also send positive affirmations like "You can do it!"

2

IT'S NOT ABOUT FOOD?!

How Food Is Involved

Health care professionals tell us that eating disorders are more about low self-esteem and self-criticism than about food. But food is definitely part of the recovery process. In order to recover from my eating disorder, I eventually had to stop bingeing, purging, and starving. Part 2 will help guide you toward a healthy relationship with food.

Dinner

E D IS A LOUSY dinner date. He is even worse than the guy who took me out to an expensive restaurant without any money, any credit cards, or any way to pay the bill (my twenty dollars just wouldn't cut it). The server held us captive in the restaurant until my date's parents arrived to bail us out. Not only does Ed never offer to pay, he is bossy and never shuts up. When I was still really struggling with my eating disorder, a typical scene in a restaurant went something like this:

> *I stare at the large menu and ask myself, "What should I order?"*
>
> *Ed mistakenly thinks I am directing this question to him and replies, "If you are absolutely determined to eat, you must at least get one of the low-fat entrées marked with the little red heart. No matter what, you must choose a lower-calorie entrée than your friend orders, which will prove that you are more in control of your life than she is."*
>
> *After my friend orders the always-forbidden cheeseburger and French fries, Ed points out, "All of that fat is going to end up right on her hips."*
>
> *"Can I order the low-fat chicken entrée that comes with a baked potato?" I ask.*
>
> *Ed says, "Fine. But on the baked potato, you will have no butter, no sour cream, no cheese, and no bacon. When the server and your friend look at you like you're nuts, just tell them that you like it better plain."*
>
> *Waiting for the food to arrive is always the hardest part. I am starving, because Ed never lets me eat any other meal on*

days that I go out to eat. All I can think about is the food. I cannot pay attention in the conversation with my friend, so I just nod in the right places and say, "Uh-huh" a lot.

Ed loves to make comments about how much fat my friend is consuming compared to me: "She's eating French fries with ketchup. Does she know how many calories are in ketchup? What's the point of pouring extra calories onto anything?"

In addition to making remarks about my friend's meal, Ed tells me exactly what to eat and how to eat it. He says, "Eat half of the chicken. But make sure you scrape off all of that fattening sauce. Cut the baked potato in half. Hide one half under your napkin and eat a few bites of the other half."

After the server clears the table, Ed congratulates me, "You did it! You are finished eating, and you are still hungry! Just think how big you would be if you had eaten that greasy hamburger! Be proud of yourself, Jenni. You have such control! Your poor friend does not have a chance in life."

Who is really in control in that scenario? It is definitely not me. Today, mealtime is a simple, enjoyable experience. I can carry on a conversation with others at the table, and no one wins an award for eating the lowest-calorie meal. Sometimes, Ed still shows up in restaurants to tell me at least a few things that I dare not eat. Last weekend, he forbade me to order my favorite food on the menu, item number four. What did I do? I ordered number four. The food was delicious, but the freedom tasted better than anything.

Be Real

"HELLO," I SAID over the phone to Heather, a woman in my therapy group. "This is Jenni. I was wondering if you have time to help me with something tonight."

Heather answered, "Sure. What's up?"

"I'm writing a very important section of my book right now. It's about not letting yourself purge when that is the only thing in the world that you want to do. I just wanted to get your perspective on some things."

After talking for a little while about how difficult it is not to purge after you have binged or even just eaten anything at all, Heather finally admitted something.

"You are not going to believe this. But just as you called, I was putting a bag of chips away. I just now finished bingeing, and the only thing that I want to do at this moment is purge."

So of course, I asked, "Are you still planning on doing it?"

"Jenni, I have to purge," Heather replied, "I have to erase everything that I just ate. I just have to."

Heather was wrong. She did not have to purge that night, and she didn't. Instead, we talked for about an hour. We talked about why purging only seemed to be the answer. We talked about separating her thoughts from Ed's. And we talked about her dreams for the future.

"Heather," I said, "Ed wants you to purge right now. What does Heather want you to do?"

Heather paused for a few seconds. She later told me that she had glanced at a bracelet on her wrist. She answered my question by reading what the ornamental letters on her bracelet spelled out, "Be real."

She continued, "Heather wants to be real."

Heather explained that this is a phrase her favorite professor always uses to inspire her to move forward in recovery. She said, "Whenever I go to a doctor's appointment, my professor tells me to be honest, to be real. She tells me that if I am real, I will make it in recovery. I will be able to leave Ed behind me."

"Well, what do you have to do tonight to be real?" I asked.

Heather knew the answer to this question, but she didn't like it at all. Finally she said, "Not purge. Ed is always the one thing in my life that keeps me from being real. He keeps me from being true to myself. Ed convinces me to chase after things that don't really exist. I know this because every time I get to where Ed wants me to go, whatever I was chasing fades off into a cloud. It's like a mirage."

"I know what you mean," I said. "Like tonight, Ed tells you that if you purge, everything will be OK. You will be at peace with yourself. You will be a success. But in reality, after you purge, you will only feel depressed, alone, and completely lost."

"Exactly," Heather said.

We talked more about what Ed wanted her to do with her life and what she wanted to do. Finally, Heather said, "I'm not going to do it. I'm not going to purge. I'm not going to let Ed disrupt my life anymore tonight. I have much more important things to do tonight and in my life than purge."

Heather chose not to purge that night. Instead, she decided to stop for a while and think. She separated herself from Ed. She thought about how Ed had lied to her before, and she knew that he was lying to her again. Heather decided to take the more difficult path that night. It would have been so easy for her to have lied to me, quickly hung up the phone, and followed all of Ed's instructions. But Heather chose to be real.

How about you? What will you choose?

Just for You

A UNT MARY SLID a plate of food in front of me and said, "I made this just for you." How many times has someone put a plate of food in front of you and said, "I made this just for you"? And did you feel as if you had to eat it? After all, it was prepared especially for you. In reality, for all you know, Aunt Mary probably tells everyone that she made her extra chocolaty chocolate layer cake just for them. But, you are hooked. You feel guilty. You have visions of the generous cook slaving over the dish in question—flour on her forehead—all just for you. And if you even dared to say those horrid words, "No thank you," you will ruin the cook's life. She will probably collapse on the spot.

The good news is you can actually say no. You don't even have to say thank you. You can just say no. If you refuse to eat that pumpkin pie that Grandma ordered from Peggy Jean's Pies especially for you, she will not die. I know this is true because I've done it, and I am still alive and so are all of the cooks that I have denied.

Recently, a friend made cookies just for me. And I turned her down. She even tried the old, "Don't you want at least one? I made them just for you." The truth is I had already eaten a good dinner, and I just didn't want to eat a cookie. The next day when the same offer for the cookies arose, I happily ate two. Why? Because I wanted a cookie. Not because Ed wanted me to eat it and not to make my friend happy. It's great to be the one in charge of when you do and don't eat cookies.

Remember, you can always politely refuse and ask the cook for a doggy bag. So the next time someone says, "I made this just for you," stop and ask yourself what you want. Be careful to distinguish between yourself and Ed. (And don't let him use this section as an excuse for you to refuse necessary nourishment.) Then, respond with a simple "yes" or "no." Whatever you say, it will not make or break the cook.

Tomorrow's newspaper headline will not read, "Jenni Says 'No' to Cream Puff Marmalade Balls: Will Aunt Betty Ever Bake Again?"

Food Plan

AFTER A COUPLE of years in recovery, I was sitting in Susan's office, and she handed me a piece of paper with a new food plan written on it.

As I looked at the food plan, Ms. Perfectionist started talking. She said, "Jenni, if you are going to follow this food plan, it is going to have to be my way. You must be perfect. There will be no room for flexibility."

I caught a glance of my future. I could see Ms. Perfectionist sitting with me at every single meal counting my carbohydrates, proteins, and more. I could see her criticizing me with each and every bite. "Are you sure that is what you need to eat? Are you sure that carbohydrate has enough carbohydrate in it?" she would say. "What if you did not put just the right amount of milk in your cereal? What if you are drinking the wrong kind of milk?"

Susan could tell that I was getting increasingly nervous as I held the food plan in my hand. So she said something that I will never forget. She said, "Throw the food plan away. Just tear it up and toss it into the trash can."

Ms. Perfectionist almost lost it. She said, "If you don't have that plan with you, how will I be able to keep you in line? How will I be able to monitor your food? How will I be able to make sure that you are doing everything perfectly?"

Susan knew that Ms. Perfectionist would have driven me crazy if I had taken the food plan home. Ms. Perfectionist would use that piece of paper as a tool to constantly berate me, insisting that I get everything just right. She would paralyze me so that I would not be able to follow the food plan at all. Susan knew all of this, so she was not about to let me take that piece of paper home with me.

In the few minutes that I held the food plan, I studied it and gained the information necessary to know what I need to eat in the course of a day to be healthy. I left Susan's office with the food plan in my head instead of my hand. That worked for me at that point in my recovery.

When I first started seeing Susan, I did not know much about nutrition and daily food requirements. Therefore, I used to carry my food plan home with me on a piece of paper. If I had not, I would never have remembered what I was supposed to eat. I even recorded what I ate every day in a food journal. This rigidity was necessary in the beginning in order to get me on the right track. But as my knowledge of nutrition grew, I no longer needed a piece of paper to tell me what to eat. In fact, combined with Ms. Perfectionist, this piece of paper could have jeopardized my recovery at one point.

The most important thing is that your food plan fits your current needs and is tailored to your personality. In order to start eating right, I highly recommend that you see a dietitian, who will know your specific food requirements. Do not be afraid to express your concerns or fears about the food plan that is presented to you. When I first began eating right, I started slowly. I was not required to eat as much as I do now. You can take your food plan one step at a time and work your way up to where you need to be.

Regardless of whether your food plan is posted on your refrigerator, stuffed in the back of your sock drawer, or thrown into a trash can, it should provide you with the knowledge of what you need to eat in the course of a day to take good care of yourself and to thoroughly neglect Ed. Even though I once threw my food plan away, I kept the knowledge it gave me. I carry that with me everywhere I go.

Cheeseburger, Please

I SAT IN ELEMENTARY school and listened as Mrs. Ferris explained the five basic food groups. As she wrote on the chalkboard, she said, "The five basic food groups are dairy products, grains, fruits, vegetables, and meat."

Ed was standing next to me. He said quietly, "This lady has no idea what she is talking about. There are really only two food groups: good and bad." And so the confusion began.

Of course, when I was a young child in that classroom, I did not realize that Ed was whispering in my ear. It is only with hindsight that I can actually see that.

For more than twenty years, Ed made it very clear to me that "good" foods were few and far between. Everything else was "bad." I was allowed to eat only the "good" foods, including apples, bagels, and pretzels. I was not allowed to touch the "bad" foods, which consisted of all sweets and desserts, anything fried, and anything with cheese, heavy cream sauce, or butter. The list goes on and on.

In my first session with Susan, she said, "There is no such thing as a bad food." Ed became increasingly irritated as she continued, "A person should not make any food illegal and should allow themselves to eat anything in moderate amounts."

When I left that session, Ed insisted on having a conversation about Susan's advice in the car on the way home.

ED: Don't listen to her. She is just like that stupid elementary teacher that talked about the alleged five food groups. Susan is just trying to confuse you and, of course, her ultimate goal is to make you fat.

JENNI: Maybe you are wrong, Ed. Susan is a professional. What benefit does she gain from lying to me?

ED: Susan is actually saying that you can eat French fries, ice cream, and even pizza. Doesn't that blow your mind?

JENNI: Yes, it does surprise me. It is definitely not what you have taught me all of these years. In fact, everything that my support team teaches me seems to be different from what I learned from you.

ED: But I am right.

JENNI: Ed, I have given you a chance for more than twenty years, and all that has gotten me is a lot of pain and suffering. It is time for me to give someone else a try.

And so I found myself in a brand-new world where all food was legal. If I felt like eating a cookie, I could eat one. This was both exciting and overwhelming. I could not believe that I could actually eat a cheeseburger—something that I had specifically denied myself for many years. But I could not just leave Susan's office that day and go out and buy a cheeseburger. No, I had to work up to that point.

Slowly I began to introduce previously forbidden foods into my lifestyle. Each time I went to the grocery store I would buy something new that I had never allowed myself to eat. Sometimes I would buy these items and they would sit at my house for a while completely wrapped in their packages—not touched. Finally, after seeing a particular food over and over again in my cabinet, I would actually add it to my food plan and eat it. I was eating things that I never thought would be possible, and I was feeling healthier than I had ever felt in my life.

Finally, the time came when I was ready to eat a cheeseburger, and I planned a special dinner with a friend for this event. Of course, Ed joined us for the meal. The server brought us menus, but I didn't need one. I knew what I wanted. Ed tried to stop me in the final moments before ordering.

He said, "Jenni, you will gain weight if you eat a cheeseburger. If you look on the menu, there are plenty of 'good' foods that you can order. You don't want to do this. You don't want to eat a cheeseburger. Trust me."

Ed had my attention as the server approached the table to take our order. The server spoke to my friend first.

Ed continued to try to change my mind, "Jenni, I have been with you for your whole life. I know what is best for you. Listen to me just like in the good ol' days when you were in such great control of your food. Don't do it!"

The server turned to me. Ed started to yell at this point, "No! No! No!" I could hear him saying this over and over in my head. He did not stop even after I had said, "Cheeseburger, please."

It is amazing, but with just those two simple words, I gained a new sense of freedom and just a little more separation from Ed. And it felt so good.

The cheeseburger didn't taste too bad either.

The Weekend with the Cake

I F I HADN'T TAKEN the cake home, it would have been thrown away and wasted. A perfectly good cake left over from an office birthday party would have been tossed into the trash can—never again to be enjoyed by anyone. Ed couldn't let that happen. And he convinced me that I couldn't let that happen. So I took it upon myself to save the cake that Friday afternoon, and I brought it home. That weekend, it was just me, Ed, and the cake.

Ed was really excited about this new tool to potentially mess up my recovery. On the drive home from work, Ed started telling me all of the options that the cake provided for us. Ed said, "You know, you could just eat a piece of cake for dinner instead of following your meal plan tonight. Or you could eat the entire cake for dinner and then follow it up with more and more food. Or you could stare at the cake all weekend and not allow yourself to eat a single bite of it. After all, it is fattening, and you really can't afford any extra calories." Ed went on and on. The possibilities with the cake were endless. At that point, I should have stopped the car and thrown the cake and Ed out the window. But I kept driving.

Even though I thought our divorce was final, I got home and struck a compromise with Ed for dinner. I told Ed that I would eat my dinner, and I would also have one piece of cake. Where's the compromise? Because I was eating a piece of cake, I didn't eat everything that I was supposed to eat for dinner. Then, the next morning, I was awakened by Ed's voice repeating, "Cake . . . eat the cake . . . cake . . . eat the cake." Ed said, "Jenni, you don't need to eat your normal balanced breakfast today. All you need to do is eat a piece of cake." Again, even though I was far along in my recovery, I shook my head and said, "OK, Ed. One piece of cake for breakfast won't hurt."

This is the story of the entire weekend. I made little compromises with Ed here and there. And I came very close to making one huge compromise. At one point over the weekend, Ed came on strong with wanting me to binge and purge. He said, "Eat the entire cake. Just do it for old time's sake. You can always purge it out of your system later." I came extremely close to obeying Ed, but I didn't. I separated myself from Ed, disagreed with him, and disobeyed him.

What I learned from the weekend with the cake is that I need to be more careful about putting myself into dangerous situations. I made a decision that I do not have to be the savior of all leftover food in the office or anywhere. This reminded me of a decision that I had made at one point in my recovery to not stock my favorite binge food in my house. Today, after lots of work in recovery, I can now keep that once-forbidden food in my refrigerator. I may even be flexible enough with eating one day to enjoy cake for breakfast without compromising my recovery. So, it's not that I will never again be able to save helpless desserts from the fate of the trash can. But for today, I am going to be cautious. Of course, Ed tells me that I am a horrible, selfish person to let such perfectly good food go to waste. But I know that my recovery is more important than a plateful of cookies or a half-eaten birthday cake. After all, an alcoholic wouldn't insist on keeping an open bottle of tequila around over the weekend. And I will no longer keep loaded guns around the house for Ed to use against me. It just makes sense.

Holidays

AMERICANS LIKE TO eat. And we use every holiday as an excuse to do just that. On the Fourth of July, we have barbecues. For birthdays, we light a cake on fire and have someone blow it out. Yes, this is a day when we actually let someone blow all over our food before we eat it. On Valentine's Day, we hope to receive a box of chocolates from our sweetheart despite the fact that we do not like half of the candies that come in the box—not to mention that we often have no idea what we are placing into our mouths until we sink our teeth into each little chocolate surprise. We let our kids wander around to random houses all over town in search of candy on Halloween. And, of course, there is Thanksgiving Day—a day in which countless people act as if they have an eating disorder whether they do or not. We like food, and we love to celebrate it.

Because holidays revolve around food, they can be really difficult for those of us with eating disorders. Ed will try to get us to make exceptions to recovery during a holiday. For instance, he might say that it is OK to starve all day on Thanksgiving so that you can stuff yourself at dinner. Ed will say it's OK to binge and purge on candy at Halloween. After all, it is only one day out of the year. It is very important that we continue on with our recovery behaviors and not let our guard down over the holidays.

While we must face food at every holiday celebration, on certain holidays, we also have other added stressors. There is no doubt that specific holidays make us busier than our regular day-to-day lives. When we have more on our plates, we are often tempted to put less effort into recovery—skipping doctors' appointments, missing therapy sessions, and not taking time to eat proper meals.

What we really need to do with the added holiday stressors from food issues to family problems is have more support in place. In reality, we need to make extra support calls and write in our journals even more than usual. We need to make a better effort to take care of ourselves. If we go the extra mile, the holiday itself will go by much more smoothly.

Each holiday gets better for me with each passing year. Thanksgiving this year was better than last year. Birthday parties at the office get easier as each one goes by. In fact, today, I actually enjoy getting together with everyone and celebrating a birthday. I do not obsess about whether or not I am allowed to have a piece of cake anymore. When it comes to the holidays, it just takes a willingness to hold onto what I have learned in recovery and a lot of practice. Take what you learn from each holiday with you to the next. As time goes by, you will think less and less about the food and stress attached to each particular day and more and more about what each holiday really means. Before you know it, you might even find yourself having a good time. Imagine that.

Overcompensating

"TABLE FOR TWO," the server called and led us to our seats. Immediately, Ed said, "You must order the lowest calorie item—garden salad with no dressing." I continued reading over the menu. I heard, "Order the highest calorie item—fettuccine Alfredo." I figured that Ed had some new tactic and was just trying to confuse me. Then I heard, "If you don't order the fettuccine Alfredo, you are anorexic." I looked up and saw that someone else had pulled up a chair.

"Counter Ed" is my new dining partner. Counter Ed encourages me to overeat in order to guarantee that I am not undereating. He forces me to eat the highest calorie items. If I do not obey Counter Ed, he claims that I am going to fall back into my eating disorder. He says, "I am here to help. It's either Ed or me."

Although Counter Ed pretends to be my ally, he is really just as controlling as Ed. With the exception of a binge, Ed will not allow me to eat anything in between meals. Counter Ed, on the other hand, will make me eat a huge snack between breakfast and lunch even if I am not hungry. He just wants to ensure that I am not restricting. Ed forces me to order a plain baked potato, while Counter Ed opts for a loaded baked potato with extra sour cream. I do not want to have to order fettuccine Alfredo any more than I want to have to order a garden salad. I want choices.

The first step in fighting Counter Ed is awareness. After I encountered this new voice, I told my support team about him. They helped me to acknowledge Counter Ed's presence and realize that he is not the solution to Ed.

I discovered that mealtime is not black and white. It is possible to eat without overeating or undereating. I stopped labeling foods as "good" and "bad." While Counter Ed is an advocate of the bad, Ed allows only the good (again with the exception of a binge where anything goes). When I quit labeling foods, both Counter Ed and Ed lost a powerful weapon. Finding the middle ground takes lots of patience and practice.

Another tool that helped me to overcome Counter Ed was planning meals ahead of time. I actually e-mailed my food plan to Thom on a daily basis. Then, I did not have to go through my day reacting to the comments, "Eat this," and, "Don't eat that." My balanced food plan was already decided, so I did not need to stress out about what to eat.

So, here's the scene: Ed and Counter Ed argue over whether I will get a salad or a hot dog, fat-free dressing or fries. They fight— I order fish. Since I get to order for myself, I actually enjoy going out to eat these days. But I have decided that any future unexpected guests need to get their own table.

Add Fat?

ADD MORE FAT to my diet? Why didn't Susan just tell me to jump off a cliff, spread my wings, and fly? Add fat? Why didn't she say, "Jenni, you need to go out, buy a gun, and rob the nearest convenience store." Add fat? She might as well have told me to print all of my best friend's deepest secrets in the *New York Times*. Add fat? It goes against my core values—against everything that I am . . . no mayo, no butter, and no regular soda.

That is how I initially felt when Susan told me that I needed to add more fat to my diet. Then I really thought about it, and I realized that adding fat does not go against my core values, but it goes against everything that Ed believes in. Ed's value system is the one that says, "A person's worth is dependent upon the amount of fat in her or his diet." My core beliefs focus on more important things like how much I value life, respect other people, and honor my friends' secrets. So, even though adding fat shakes Ed's entire sense of being, it doesn't have to disrupt my world.

I will admit that I practically have a second B.S. (and I do mean B.S.) degree in how to avoid fat in my diet. But I also have a real degree in biochemistry, which tells me that my body actually needs fat in order to function properly. For instance, fat is an essential component in the membranes of every single cell in my body. Also, not eating enough fat tends to set me up for bingeing. After going a long period of time without eating enough fat, I usually end up bingeing on lots of high-fat items—because my body needs fat.

So, today, I am taking a step into the unknown world of fat. The next time I go into a restaurant I might actually get to use my butter knife! And maybe I will choose real ice cream over frozen yogurt on occasion. I might even toss my "I Can't Believe It's Not

Butter" spray and buy something that I really can believe is butter. Adding fat is an adventure into a new world. It actually might be fun.

Whether it is fun or not, it is definitely terrifying. As I write this, Ed is painting a horrible portrait in my mind of what I will look like after I add more fat to my diet. I actually kind of agree with Ed at this point. But I am still going to disobey him. In my years of experience in agreeing with Ed, he usually ends up being wrong when all is said and done. So, I am sure that he is wrong about this, too.

Add fat? Yes, I am going to do it. In fact, I am about to go to the grocery store to stock up on those items that I have never purchased. I will get to explore grocery aisles that I have never walked down before. Of course, Ed will be kicking and screaming the entire way. I'll just distract him by encouraging him to play his favorite grocery store game—analyzing the items in every other person's grocery cart. While he stares at the woman in aisle three putting a bag of microwave popcorn into her cart, I will choose 2 percent over skim milk. While he determines whether the man in aisle four will buy corn flakes or Froot Loops, I will buy cheese and peanut butter. While Ed tries to count the exact number of regular sodas in the young boy's cart in aisle seven, I will live my life.

I remember sitting in my dietitian's office one day. I said, "Susan, I don't understand why I need to add more fat to my diet. I could survive another fifty years without adding more fat."

Susan replied, "Maybe. Maybe not. But even so, it's not about surviving. It's about living."

Overboard

FIRST, SHE MARCHED me out to the edge of the plank. Then, she told me to take the next step in my recovery, which sent me soaring through the air to the murky water below. This is how I felt when Susan said, "It's time for you to move from your food plan to intuitive eating." She seemingly tossed my food plan out the window and told me that I needed to start listening to my body signals. I depended on my food plan and was not sure that I could make it on my own. This was different from the time when Susan told me to throw my food plan into the trash can. In that instance, she wanted me to keep the knowledge of the food plan in my head instead of on a piece of paper. Now she wanted me to forget about the food plan altogether and do something called "intuitive eating."

When I fell overboard, Ed was waiting in a lifeboat ready to save me. He urged, "Hop on in. Obviously, Susan doesn't care about you, but I'm still here." I refused Ed's attempts to "help" and frantically treaded water for one week—the time period between appointments with Susan.

At that next visit, I explained to Susan that I didn't like swimming all that much. She said that there had been a misunderstanding; I was not really supposed to throw out my food plan. Susan admitted that she should not have used the words, "Move from your food plan to intuitive eating." Instead, she said, "You need to keep your food plan and simply add body signals to it." I needed to both use the knowledge of my food plan and listen to my body. I was still supposed to follow my food plan, but I needed to learn how to make adjustments as necessary based on my body signals. For instance, if I still felt hungry after finishing a meal, I needed to eat an additional serving of fruit, protein, or whatever I desired. Knowing that I was not abandoning my food plan made all the difference in the world to me.

So, I didn't need Ed's lifeboat after all. In fact, I stopped panicking out there in the water, put my feet down, and realized that I could stand.

Food Accounting 101

AT 5:30 P.M., the burrito pan was half full. One hour later it was empty. And I cannot account for any of the missing burritos. This sloppy food accounting would not have occurred years ago. Ed trained me well, and each burrito would have been accounted for. It would be something like this: Christina ate one and one-half burritos. Bob took three burritos, ate two, and threw one away. Lindsey took one burrito and ate three-fourths of it. But, not today. Today, the whereabouts of a large number of burritos is unknown.

OK, I will admit that prior to the last sighting of the burritos at 5:30 P.M., I was aware of the food distribution at the party. Because prior to 5:30 P.M., Ed was acting as if he were my date. I sipped a Diet Coke, glared at the large assortment of food, and took note of what everyone else was eating. This far into recovery, Ed has new tactics to keep food at bay. Tonight, it was one of his new favorites, "Nothing here fits into your food plan." Ed actually acts as if he supports my food plan and uses it against me. And of course, with Ed, it's all or nothing. He doesn't say that items X and Y don't fit into my food plan. No, he says the entire assortment of five large spreads of food does not fit into my food plan. And, of course, he uses the old standard, "Besides, if you eat any of this, you'll be fat tomorrow." For about thirty minutes, I listened to Ed. Then, I realized what I was doing.

I was hungry. I walked over to the food, and I ate a reasonable amount. I didn't try to show Ed who was boss by eating a huge amount of food. And after I ate, I had a great time. The party became about the people, and the food became part of the background. That's when I lost track of the burritos.

Thom's Turn

1. Sharing Your Food Plan

Included in the e-mail I receive every day are messages from colleagues, friends, clients, readers, and of course the requisite junk mail. And sometimes I receive a daily menu. Jenni was the first to do this, and now many others have benefited from the idea. When she is having a particularly difficult time with food, Jenni will still e-mail her food plan for the day, detailing specifically what she plans to eat that day. Usually she will do this for several days in a row until she feels on solid recovery ground again.

By writing out a food plan and sending it to someone you trust, you make it harder for Ed to inch his way back into a controlling position in your life—or you make it harder for him to remain in control if he has already gotten a foothold. By sharing your food plan with someone, you are demonstrating a willingness to take care of yourself at least for that one day. Even if you don't adhere to the food plan perfectly, you will still be making an important stand against Ed and for you.

2. Sharing a Binge

I worked with Jenni for close to a year before I could get her to share with me exactly what she had eaten during a binge. I knew that sharing this information with me would relieve some of the shame associated with her bingeing. But Jenni always thought that she was the best bulimic around. She was convinced that her binges were "bigger and badder" than anything I had previously come across. She thought that I would be so astonished by the large amount of food that she had eaten that I would look down on her, that I would realize I was in over my head, and maybe that I would give up on her. She was of course wrong about all of this.

Finally, Jenni brought in her food journal, which detailed many binges. She let me read a typical binge out of her journal while she sat in my office with a blanket over her head to hide her embarrassment. To Jenni's surprise, the documentation of her binge looked very normal to me. Once she was convinced that I was telling her the truth, Jenni admitted that she felt less shame and more at peace with herself in regard to her eating behaviors.

Whether a binge for you is the size of a "normal" meal or the size of ten meals combined, you might find it helpful to write down what you have eaten and share it with someone on your support team. The unconditional love and acceptance that you will feel far outweighs any initial embarrassment about the binge itself. And if you think you are the best bulimic around, remember, that honor belongs to Jenni.

3. Your Relationship with Food

In recovery, you will need to establish a specific model for your healthy relationship with food. Make a list of any healthy aspects of your relationship with food that you already have in place. Some healthy aspects of Jenni's relationship with food when she first began recovery were as follows:

1. I include a wide variety of fruits and vegetables in my diet.
2. I enjoy sharing meals with my friends and family.
3. I sometimes allow myself to eat dessert.

Make another list of all of the problems that you have with food. Some of Jenni's problems with food were the following:

1. Sometimes I eat past the point of hunger and binge on a huge amount of food.
2. I generally do not allow any fat in my diet.
3. I enjoy cooking for others, but I never eat anything that I prepare.

This may seem like a lot to ask, but it is very important that you be specific and comprehensive in your listing.

Create a vision of a healthy, recovering relationship with food. Describe it in detail, and list specific examples of healthy eating. If you work with a food plan, include the food plan in your vision. If you do not work with a food plan, write a menu for a healthy eating day as an example.

Now here comes the real challenge. Eat according to your healthy vision for the next two days. If that seems like too much, try just one day.

Here are a couple of ideas around food that Ed surely won't like: 1) For greater accountability (similar to exercise 1), many people find it helpful to take a photo of their plate before mealtimes and send it via text message to a trusted person. Some send a follow-up text as well—after eating. 2) Recovery Record mobile app enables you to track your progress with food and even syncs the information you collect— about food and feelings—with your therapist's account (that is, if he or she uses the app, too).

3

MIRROR, MIRROR ON THE WALL

Is Thin Really Everything?

Eating disorders are characterized by excessive concern about one's physical appearance, especially in terms of size and weight. There was a time when I considered being thin more important than anything. Now I know that there is much more to life than being a size 0. Part 3 will help you break away from constant criticism of your appearance and prepare you to explore real meaning in your life.

You Don't Look Like
You Have an Eating Disorder

I WAS TOLD THAT he was a leading expert in eating disorder treatment, a medical doctor with many years' experience, currently the director of eating disorder services in a prestigious hospital. He was the first health care professional that I saw after finally admitting to myself that I did have a problem with food. You can imagine the struggle I had gone through to convince myself to take this drastic step.

When I walked into his office, this expert doctor said the very worst thing that he could possibly have said to me. He said, "You don't look like you have an eating disorder."

Now that I have been in recovery for many years, I realize just how unprofessional, ignorant, and dangerous that comment was—especially coming from an "expert." First of all, at the time that I walked into his office, I met all of the diagnostic criteria for anorexia, including the weight requirement, but that was not thin enough for this doctor. Didn't he realize that such a comment could send me over the edge (or more accurately, under the edge)?

Second and most important, there is no particular body shape or appearance that someone must have in order to qualify for having an eating disorder. Anyone—male or female—of any race, age, height, or weight can have an eating disorder. The girl who lives down the street may be anorexic; the grocery store clerk may be bulimic. It does not matter what someone looks like on the outside.

Many people with eating disorders do not seek help, because they do not feel as if they look sick enough to have an eating disorder. The truth is that some of the most dangerously ill girls in my support group at one time or another were the girls who appeared to be at a "normal" weight. In fact, I was at my very worst as far as my eating disorder behaviors are concerned when I was at a "normal" weight as compared to when I was extremely underweight.

I specifically do not include any "before" pictures in this book of what I looked like prior to recovery, because I do not want people using my pictures to disqualify themselves from treatment. Some people may think that they have to look just as I did in order to get help. I encourage you not to compare yourself to pictures of those with eating disorders on television or in magazines. It goes without saying that Ed will tell you that you are not thin enough to have an eating disorder. He says that to all of us.

Just the other day, a girl in my support group was talking about her first visit to a new psychotherapist. The first words out of his mouth were, "You don't look like you have an eating disorder."

It is no wonder that we get so confused about whether or not we have eating disorders when so many professionals seem to lack the knowledge that people with eating disorders come in all shapes and sizes.

Eating disorders are really about excessive control, painful perfectionism, and stubborn self-hatred. They are not about whether or not your thighs touch, the width of your hips, the size of your butt, or the number on a scale. Unfortunately, anorexia, bulimia, and related disorders exist at every number on the scale. Eating disorders do not discriminate. Ed will be happy to destroy your life at whatever size and weight you happen to be.

Don't give him the chance.

The Scale

IN THE FOURTH grade, I stood in a long line with my classmates waiting to be weighed by the school nurse. After my friend Sandi was weighed, the nurse called out, "76 pounds." I was next in line and extremely nervous. What if the nurse called out some horribly large number? Then, my entire class would know my secret. They would know that I was fat. I slowly stepped onto the large metal contraption. One foot. Two feet. The nurse seemed to take forever as she adjusted the scale.

I just kept thinking, "Make up your mind," as she slowly determined the fate of my life. Finally, she yelled, "76 pounds." I quietly tapped the nurse on the shoulder and told her that she had made a mistake. Sandi was the one who weighed 76 pounds—not me. Agitated, the nurse looked me straight in the eye and said, "Don't you think I know how to use a scale, young lady? You weigh 76 pounds. Now move along." How is it possible that I could weigh the same as Sandi? We were the same height, but between the two of us, she had always been the thin one. I was the fat one. Yet the scale proved otherwise. The scale told me I was thin. It told me that I was a good person. That's when the scale and I became such good friends.

Needless to say, Ed was ecstatic about my new friendship. I eventually started every day with the scale. If the number on the scale was too high, Ed told me that I was a sorry excuse for a human being. I was a failure. But if Ed liked the number, he boosted my ego. He said, "You are such a success! You are in such control of your life!" Aside from telling me whether or not I was a good person, Ed used the number on the scale to determine what I was allowed to eat during the day. A high number called for restriction.

If the number was low enough and if Ed was in a particularly good mood, I might be allowed to eat a snack after school or maybe even a dessert.

When I began recovery, I quickly called it quits with the scale. Ed did not take our breakup well. He yelled, "What will I do without my favorite tool? How will I control you?" (I admit that Ed found other ways to control me, but none was so powerful as the scale.) In addition to giving up the scale, I decided that I no longer wanted anyone to tell me my weight. I would let my doctor weigh me only with the understanding that I did not want to know the number. I did not want to be accidentally told my weight by a new nurse. I did not want to overhear the doctor and nurse talking about my weight. And I did not want my medical chart to be put in a place where I—or Ed—could potentially read my weight. So as I gained weight in recovery, I never knew how much or how little. This strategy worked best for me. Talk with your support team to determine what is best for you.

I have absolutely no idea what I weigh today. It is such a freedom. As you may know, no matter what the number is on the scale, Ed will attempt to use it against you. The number can never be too low. And sometimes one-fourth of a pound is too much—or too little. Today, the only things I weigh are the pros and cons in making a decision. When it came to giving up the scale in my life, the pros far outweighed the cons. And that was a decision that I did not take lightly.

Fat

WHEN I VISIT my internist, Dr. Tucker, he says, "You don't need to gain or lose a pound. You are the perfect weight."

Ed undoubtedly interjects, "Dr. Tucker is an idiot. You will only be the 'perfect' weight when he tells you that you need to gain fifty pounds. Face it. You're fat."

Do I trust Ed or Dr. Tucker? I put my faith in the man who spent years in medical school analyzing the human body and who devotes his entire life to helping people achieve maximum health. (Ed could never pass the medical school admissions test, and he devotes no time to making sure that my heart is still pumping.) In other words, I trust Dr. Tucker. Dr. Tucker's role on my support team is to have complete authority over my weight. Throughout recovery, my weight has fluctuated greatly. Sometimes Dr. Tucker said that I needed to gain weight, and at other times, he said that my weight was just fine. At any weight, Dr. Tucker has encouraged me to keep moving forward in recovery. He has helped me make necessary adjustments to my food plan in order to maintain optimum health. What a relief it is to have Dr. Tucker supervise my weight! I no longer have to worry about whether or not I am fat. I simply put my faith in Dr. Tucker and believe what he tells me.

Does this mean that when I look in a mirror, I say, "Jenni, you are just so thin?" Of course not. Ed is inside every mirror pointing out all of my cellulite, flab, and jiggling. And I often see the illusion of fat. I not only trust Dr. Tucker's opinion over Ed's comments, but I also trust Dr. Tucker over my very own eyesight. When I see fat, I know that I am not fat.

Does this mean that I never feel fat? No. Thom believes that it is actually beneficial for me to "feel fat." A true test of my recovery has been feeling overweight and still eating breakfast, lunch, and dinner. Thom says that simultaneously following my food plan and feeling fat proves that my recovery is very strong. Regardless of how I feel, Dr. Tucker is in control of the scale, and he keeps the number to himself. I do not need to know specific digits to know that I am healthy.

My Private Platoon

M Y MOTHER WOULD have been disappointed if she had known about the men in my closet. Among them were Private Calvin Klein, Private Gap, and Private Wrangler. They were my wardrobe, and they fought the wars in my life. They answered to Sergeant Ed and existed for my protection. Ed said, "Your private platoon will ensure that you are never a failure. But if you ever lose these guys, you will be a worthless nobody."

All I had to do to keep my platoon around me was to stay extremely thin. Private Klein insisted on my being a size 0, and Private Gap mandated that I remain an extra-extra-small. Private Wrangler allowed me to be a size 1, but it was a "small" size 1. If I stayed thin enough, they would stay and fight my battles. If I did less than perfect on an exam in college, they fought to prove that I was not a failure. If I forgot the words of a song in a performance, they affirmed that I was still a wonderful singer. As long as I fit into them, I was thin. I was good. Nothing else really mattered.

If I gained weight, Sergeant Ed warned that he would order my platoon to go AWOL. Without them, if I failed an exam, I was stupid. If I made a mistake in a song, I would never be a successful singer. If I was not thin enough, my safety net would disappear.

After being in recovery, I realized that Ed was not commanding my platoon to fight *for* me but against me. I was slowly being strangled, so I, not Ed, transferred my platoon to a nearby thrift store. And I did one of the most difficult things that I have had to do in recovery. I went shopping and bought clothes that fit my new, healthy body. Today, I have a wardrobe that conforms to me. I don't need to change myself for a particular dress or pair of slacks anymore. And my new clothes don't protect me from anything except the weather. Among my clothes is my favorite pair of jeans by Old Navy. Despite the name, I am not keeping any sailors in my closet. I have had enough of the military.

Skinny Jenni

AT ONE BUSINESS on Music Row in Nashville, I was known as Skinny Jenni. Whenever I walked into that building, I was bombarded with, "Hi, Skinny Jenni," "How's it going, Skinny Jenni?" and "What can we do for you, Skinny Jenni?" I was known for my emaciated body. I was Skinny Jenni and proud of it.

When I first began recovery, I put my singing career on hold and focused all of my energy on getting better. Because I was not writing songs, I did not enter that particular business for about two years.

When I finally did go into that building again, I walked in as a whole new woman—a healthy and happy Jenni. As I sat in the reception area waiting for my appointment, someone walked by and said, "Hi, Skinny Jenni." Immediately, the receptionist looked at me with a confused expression and said, "Why in the world would anyone call you Skinny Jenni?" Of course, my self-esteem immediately hit the floor, and Ed roared with laughter. He said, "See, you're not skinny anymore. You're fat. If you follow me, I can help you earn back your title, Skinny Jenni."

After taking a few seconds to compose myself, I responded to this all-too-sensitive receptionist, "I have an eating disorder. The last time I was in here I weighed much less than I do now. Now, I am in recovery and doing great." The young woman did not know how to react to my honest answer, so she quickly began working on her computer and shuffling papers around her desk.

After my appointment was over, I immediately made a support call to Morgan, because I didn't want Ed to be able to take advantage of this situation. I explained the incident with the receptionist to Morgan. I told her how I had originally taken the woman's comment as an incredible insult. Then, after thinking briefly about how amazing my life is without Ed, I was able to gain my confidence and speak the truth. Today, I am thrilled that I am no longer remembered by the size of my body. When I was lost in anorexia, being thin was all that mattered to me. And I guess that emanated from me, because that is what people thought of when they thought of Jenni.

Now, when people think of me, I hope other words come to mind—words like *energetic*, *full of life*, and *caring*. Ed still tries to get me back now and then by suggesting that *fat* is the word that comes to people's minds when they think of me, but I don't buy it. I am so much more than a body size. And so are you.

Reaching out to Morgan in this situation made all the difference. If picking up the phone to make a support call is sometimes too difficult for you, maybe you can at least send a short text—like "SOS" or even "Ed." Tell your support team ahead of time what your distress signal text might say, and let them know helpful ways to respond.

Impurities

I F YOU POUR water through an expensive filter, you don't expect it to come out brown. Although I would never install a faulty purifier on my faucet, for years, I depended on another type of defective filter in my life. His name is Ed. He is a reverse filter—contaminating rather than purifying. And he pollutes words. A sentence enters Ed's ears, and an interpretation flies out of his mouth.

If someone tells me, "You look healthy," Ed spits out, "You are a big fat pig." He derives the same meaning from "You have great curves," and even "Your teeth are beautiful." Ed turns a friend's compliment about my hair into, "You're definitely a big fat pig." When my first psychiatrist told me, "You don't look like you have an eating disorder," Ed laughed and said, "You are such a big fat pig." When my current support team says, "You are doing so well," Ed explains that what they are really trying to say is, "We've turned you into a big fat pig."

No matter what combination of words enters Ed's ears, the equivalent of dirty, cloudy water always pours out. In recovery, I finally learned to throw out my filter altogether. Today, I actually take people's words at face value. If a friend says, "Great coat," I assume that she really likes my coat. I have always expected others to believe me when I speak, and, now, I give the same respect.

When Ed is really tempting me to give our marriage another shot, I find it helpful to ask clarifying questions instead. For instance, I will say to a friend, "When you said, 'You look great,' I heard that I am fat. What did you mean?" To this day, the answer to that question has never included the description of an overweight barnyard animal.

Miss Anorexic

NOTHING COMPARES TO the support provided to me from the girls in my eating disorder therapy group. And nothing is quite like the competition I feel with each of them. It's not a competition between who can give the best support, who is doing the best in recovery, or who has the prettiest face. No, points in this competition are awarded for eating the least amount of food, starving for the longest period of time, and losing the most weight. Bonus points go to the person who achieves the smallest number on the scale.

Within a few seconds of walking into group therapy for the first time, Ed sized everyone up. He gave me a quick analysis of who was smaller and who was larger than me. Ed said, "The girls who are thinner than you are just plain better than you." He said that the girls who had been hospitalized and tube fed were stronger than I was, because they were more successful at starving. Ed told me that I should be more like the girl who eats only one apple per day.

I have now realized that the competition is not between the girls and me, it is among all of our different Eds. While we spend an hour and a half each Monday night helping each other stay on the road to recovery, our Eds bicker back and forth about who weighs the least. When Amy calls me and says that she hasn't eaten in two days, I offer support and words of encouragement, and Ed tells me that I should be jealous of her self-control. As long as I recognize that Ed, not Jenni, wants me to be crowned Miss Anorexic, I can remain strong in recovery and provide support to the girls who need me.

Recently, Ed told me that I could not go out with the girls on Saturday night, because I was fat.

He said, "Jenni, all of the girls going out tonight are skinnier than you. You will be the fattest one there."

At first, I agreed with Ed, "You're right. I'll spend the whole night being jealous of their body sizes. I will be miserable."

Then, I remembered that Ed is the one who runs the competition for the best anorexic, not me. So I went out with my friends. Ed spent the evening trying to figure out who had the smallest arms, who was wearing the smallest size clothing, and who ate the least for dinner. Of course, Ed shares all of this information with me, but I don't give his ideas a second thought. Instead, I concentrate on what really matters. I laugh. I listen. I live.

You Must Be Thin

WHEN I WAS seven years old, I sat in a circle with the other girls in my dance class and listened to the instructor explain the importance of being thin. She told us how we should eat, and she taught us exercises that would help us tone those flabby parts of our bodies. I was only seven years old.

I learned at a young age that being a performer meant I had to look good. Aside from people like my dance instructor directly telling me this, I could see it for myself in magazines, on television, and in movies. Actresses, models, and singers all seemed to have thinner bodies than any of the women I actually came across in my everyday life. Ed helped me to achieve this superhuman body; I became thinner than everyone I knew. Ed told me that I could, now, succeed in music.

I am no longer as thin as I used to be, but I am still a performer, trying to make it in the music industry. Ed takes every chance he gets to tell me that I won't succeed due to my body size. So, what do I do?

I keep doing what I know is right. I follow both my food and exercise plans. I try not to obsess about my weight, and I feel great. I also look for role models in the media who have healthy bodies. One of these individuals is Cindy Crawford. She is one of the most successful models of all time, and she is a normal weight. Crawford has even been labeled as "fat" by her rail-thin peers. Like her, I strive to be a positive role model.

The funny thing is that when I was extremely thin, my voice was anything but ideal. I didn't have the strength to hit high notes. I didn't have the lung capacity to carry out phrases. And I didn't have the ability to put emotion into my music. I was simply the hollow shell of what looked like the perfect singer. I definitely did not have the ability to focus long enough to actually write a song. I started to write so many songs when I was in the depths of my eating disorder. Only now have I been able to finish any of those lyrics.

Today, I can really sing. I can really write. And people tell me that I look great. Sure, they no longer tell me, "Oh, you are just so thin." But they don't tell that to Cindy Crawford either. And I can handle that. I recently took the best head shots that I have ever had in my life. There is color in my face and life in my eyes. The most common remark I used to receive about my previous "eating disordered" head shots was, "You look like you are on drugs." (What they were seeing was a woman in an abusive relationship—with Ed.) That's not exactly the image I want to portray to record labels. Today, I can present my whole self to record labels—a strong, healthy woman who has the depth to write real songs and actually has the energy to sing them. And I like that.

Lindsey

PEOPLE ALWAYS ASK me how old I was when I developed my eating disorder. I say, "For as long as I can remember, I did not allow myself to eat certain foods. And I cannot remember a time when I did not think that I was fat." But after today, I know that there must have been a point in my life when I was perfectly satisfied with my body.

I spent the day baby-sitting an eighteen-month-old girl. I was giving her a bath, and I noticed how she reacted to her body, how she looked at her arms and legs, and how she treated herself. She is a beautiful, healthy girl, and like most children her age, she has a cute round stomach. I watched her as she played with her belly. She would wet her hands and caress her stomach, spreading the water all over herself. As she did this, she was smiling and having fun. She was not disgusted with her round belly; she was not pinching the fat around her stomach and wishing she could somehow cut it off of her body. She accepts her body and is fascinated by each and every part. I like to think that this is how I was as an eighteen-month-old.

And I believe that my body image can one day be like that again. Every day I am getting closer to that kind of self-acceptance. I have moments when I am really excited to be a woman and to actually have curves on my body. And now that I am eating right and exercising in a healthy way, I am beginning to feel comfortable in my body. I like the strength that I feel in my legs when I walk. When I was starving myself, I used to feel weak all of the time— as if I could be carried away by the wind. Today I stand with confidence.

At what age will Lindsey start agonizing over her body? When will she first understand the word *fat*? I watch her and hope that she will never be in the grips of a deadly eating disorder. As long as people like you are becoming educated about eating disorders and are reaching out for help, I believe that young children today can grow up in a society that focuses more on health than on weight— a world that does not consider appearance to be the most crucial aspect of identity. The next generation might not have to wage a war against their bodies, because we are making changes to ourselves today. Right now.

Illusion

"OBJECTS IN MIRROR are closer than they appear." I never had a problem believing this text imprinted on my car mirror. But I could not believe the professionals that told me, "When you look at your body, it is not as it appears." I knew that eating disorders were associated with body image problems, and I knew that I had an eating disorder. Nonetheless, when it came to my body, I could see just fine. And I saw fat. Ed completely agreed with me. He would say, "You can read the bottom row on the eye chart. Don't believe those lies about illusions. You see fat, because you are fat." To Ed's dismay, I finally had an experience that convinced me otherwise.

Recently, I was at a friend's house looking at myself in her wall-to-wall mirror. The mirror was so big that I could not help but see myself in it. Anyway, the girl looking back at me appeared fat. On the very next day, I was standing in the same exact place looking into that huge mirror again, but the person looking back at me was not the same. She looked great—definitely not fat. I was amazed, because only twenty-four hours earlier, this girl was positively fat. At this point, Ed tried to convince me that I had miraculously lost thirty pounds overnight. You know, the further along I get in recovery, the less sense Ed makes. I didn't buy it, and I knew without a doubt that I do, in fact, see an illusion when I look into the mirror.

Now, when I look at my body, I remember that objects in a mirror are not always as they appear. Ed disagrees: "Your eyesight is 20/20, and your thighs are fat." In these moments, I am grateful that I have given Dr. Tucker the complete responsibility of evaluating my body size. He says that my weight is "perfect" and I do not need to lose a pound. Nevertheless, when I pass by a mirror, I can't help but think about what I need to lose. And it's not weight; it's Ed.

Thin

WHEN I WAS in the depths of my eating disorder, "I'm thin" used to be my answer to all of life's tough questions. Am I happy? Yes, I'm thin. Am I a good performer? Sure, I'm thin. Am I confident? Of course, I'm thin. As long as I was thin, I did not really have to think about anything else. And because I was starving myself, I could not think straight anyway. Now that I look back at those years, I realize that my obsession with being thin kept me lost in a fog.

My size was the only thing that I thought I could completely control. I agonized over the thought of gaining weight. I would stand in front of the mirror and wonder how I could avoid ever gaining one pound. If I gained one pound, I was a failure. If my clothes started fitting tighter, it meant I had no control. It meant I would have to focus on other areas of my life and actually acknowledge my imperfections.

Being in recovery sometimes means gaining weight. But I don't view gaining weight as a failure. In fact, the opposite is true. Gaining weight is a triumph. It means I am free of my struggle to control my size. Because my size no longer runs my life, I am able to focus on other issues. I actually risk the possibility of failing at something. I am grateful for this ability to take risks.

Today, I am more involved with my life and in tune with my real dreams. I don't live in a haze where I think everything is just peachy—as I slowly kill myself. The fog has lifted, and the world truly seems brighter. When I go outside, I notice things that I had never seen before—leaves changing colors in the fall, the first flowers of springtime, and a little rabbit that lives in my backyard. And when I go inside—into my mind—I see passions, fears, and questions that I had never seen in the past. I still don't have the perfect answers to all of life's questions, but, now, I know that the answers have nothing to do with, "I'm thin."

Vampire

THERE IS NOTHING better than sorting through your mail and finding a letter from an old friend stuck between this month's phone bill and another "You Might Be a Winner!" postcard. And there is nothing worse than opening that letter and discovering that your friend enclosed photographs of you. These are the moments when I wish I were a vampire. Vampires don't have reflections and don't leave images on film. If I were a vampire, I could look into store windows without the fear of catching a glimpse of myself. If I were a vampire, I wouldn't have to watch myself in Dad's home movies. If I were a vampire, I wouldn't have to stare at the grimy floor in a public restroom in order to avoid the mirrors.

Of course, there would be some drawbacks to being a vampire. I couldn't do a quick mirror check to see if there was something left over from lunch between my teeth. If I were a vampire, I would really have to trust my hairdresser. And without a photo ID, I could forget about driving or traveling. Above all, if I were a vampire, I would not be as healthy as I am now.

A huge part of my recovery has been reconnecting to my body. To do this, I had to stop avoiding my reflection in mirrors. I had to really look at my body and accept what I see. An important recovery tool has actually been standing directly in front of a mirror and looking at myself. I finally realized that the purpose of a mirror is not to reveal who is skinnier—the hottest new singer on the market or me. And a mirror is not a tool created to determine whether I am a good or bad person. Being a vampire would have been a great excuse for me to stay in my eating disorder. Luckily, I never did grow fangs. I never liked the whole sucking blood concept anyway.

Thom's Turn

1. The Master Hypnotist

As you are reading this, allow your attention to drift down to your left foot. Focus all of your attention on your left foot. Just your left foot. Imagine that your left foot is becoming heavy. Very heavy. Notice every sensation that you feel in your left foot. Your left foot continues to become heavier and heavier. Read slowly and pause between sentences to increase your attention on your left foot. It is becoming very heavy. Eventually you won't even be able to lift it.

What did you notice as you read the previous paragraph? Were you hypnotized into experiencing your left foot as growing heavy? Did you resist the suggestions? Either way, you were thinking of your left foot. Even if you say to yourself, "I will not think of my left foot," guess what? Try this: don't think of a purple elephant. Don't think of the color green.

You may not think so, but people are easily hypnotized. And Ed is a master hypnotist. He hypnotizes you into thinking that you are fat. Just as the previous paragraph had you thinking of your left foot, feeling it becoming heavier, Ed focuses your attention on all the various aspects of your body that make you feel uncomfortable. "Feel the waistline of your pants," is one of his favorites. He makes you believe that you are larger than you really are. He makes you feel it, and he makes you see it when you look in the mirror—just like the master hypnotist that he is.

Your left foot did not really become heavier in this exercise, and you are really not as large as Ed makes you feel. (And it is Ed who is objecting to this idea right now. Do you hear him?) Write down the hypnotic suggestions that Ed repeats to you over and over again. Keep the list around; add to it as you become more aware of

Ed's hypnotic suggestions. The list in your pocket or purse can serve as a reminder that you have been in Ed's trance.

2. Baby Pictures

Jenni tells me that there is a picture of a little baby taped to her bathroom mirror. This is a picture of herself. She taped it on her mirror as a tool to fight Ed.

When Jenni looks in the mirror, Ed always tells her exactly what he thinks about her appearance. "You are fat," he says. Jenni used to believe what Ed said; she would look at herself and say, "Yes, you are fat." Now, when Jenni hears Ed's voice as she looks in the mirror, she glances at the photo of the little girl. To this day, Jenni has never been able to look at the little girl and tell her that she is fat. In fact, Jenni even protects the little girl from Ed's comments. She says, "You are wrong, Ed. I am not fat." The picture inspires Jenni to take care of herself in spite of Ed's criticism.

Find a picture of yourself as small child. Tape it to your bathroom mirror, or find a frame and put it on your bedside table. Try saying to the child in the photo what Ed says to you. You may have a difficult time telling the innocent little child that she is fat, ugly, or worthless. Or maybe you can. Jenni immediately had difficulty with this, but many clients have easily insulted the childhood version of themselves. (It's just an outward demonstration of what goes on internally all the time.) Either way, there is something very important for you to learn here. Challenge yourself to recognize how Ed abuses the child within you, and practice stepping up to protect that child.

3. Powerful Clothes

During one therapy session with Jenni, my office was covered with jeans. There were jeans on the floor, jeans on the couch, and jeans slung over the chairs in my office. These were Jenni's anorexic jeans, jeans that Jenni had worn when she was still married to Ed. These jeans, representing sickness and depression, no longer fit Jenni's body. It had taken a long time, but Jenni was finally determined that these jeans were not going to fit into her life anymore either.

When these jeans were in Jenni's closet, they talked to her day and night. They said, "You are fat." They said, "If you just lose a little bit of weight, you could wear me again," and "You are a loser, because you are too big to fit into me." Jenni did not want her clothes to have that much power over her, but it still took her a while to decide to get rid of them.

Jenni brought all of her anorexic jeans to my office, and we spent an entire therapy session saying good-bye to her jeans. Jenni told me stories associated with each pair. We took out a plastic toy ray gun, and Jenni zapped the jeans in order to symbolically take away some of the power that they had over her. By the end of the session, the jeans had lost their power. They had simply become clothes that did not fit. After the session, Jenni loaded all of the jeans in her car and took them directly to the thrift store.

To people who don't understand eating disorders this may seem silly, but if you have an eating disorder, you know exactly what I am talking about. You have clothes that talk to you, right?

Go through your closet and find the clothes that have power over you. Gather them up and take them to a therapy session. Or choose a trusted friend with whom you can talk about your clothes. You are not unusual if this seems like too much to ask initially. So be creative. Maybe put your "powerful clothes" in a box and leave it in the trunk of your car for a while. Maybe you will be willing to leave them with a friend. I have one client who has stored some of her anorexic clothes in a closet in our group therapy room. We all know they are there, and we will eventually celebrate when she decides to get rid of them.

Be respectful of yourself when you are doing difficult things like this, but also be firm. Get rid of those powerful clothes and discover the freedom that comes with what Jenni refers to as her "quiet closet."

4

MERRY-GO-ROUND

The Nuts and Bolts of Recovery

Sometimes the cycle of bingeing, purging, and starving seems end-less. In order to break free from this cycle, I learned to stay true to my goals; I learned to get up each time I fell down; I learned to never give up. As I added new recovery tools, Ed would attack me from all angles. But as long as I continued separating from Ed, I was able to stand my ground. Part 4 takes you through some of my specific learning experiences that enabled me to finally divorce Ed. I hope that you can learn by example and not have to go through as much turmoil with Ed as I did.

Ed's Defense Attorney

I ALMOST WENT TO medical school. I never even came close to attending law school, so why do I so often find myself acting as Ed's defense attorney? When I am arguing with other people about body image or eating issues, I sometimes realize that I am actually defending Ed.

For instance, I told another girl, Stephanie, in my therapy group, "I just feel fat all of the time."

Stephanie replied, "Jenni, you know that you do not judge your body size correctly. You are not fat by any means."

Ed quickly stood up and was prepared to dispute those facts when I hastily pushed him aside and said, "I am fat. I can't fit into any of my old clothes. Even my 'fat' jeans are too small now. This all means that I am without a doubt fat."

Looking back on that situation, I see that I was clearly standing in Ed's corner doing his fighting for him. I am sure that he was patting me on the back saying, "Right on. Right on, Jenni." I probably even gave him one or two high fives throughout that conversation. And that situation has happened more than once. I remember a conversation with my dietitian.

I explained to Susan, "I ate out at a restaurant for lunch, so I am just going to eat a bowl of cereal for dinner tonight."

Susan replied, "You need to stick to your meal plan. One bowl of cereal just won't cut it for dinner."

Once again, I spoke as Ed's representative: "I honestly will not be hungry for dinner after eating such a big lunch. A bowl of cereal will satisfy me just fine. That is all I need. I don't want to eat a big dinner if I am not hungry."

Today I am more aware of my tendency to defend Ed, and I stop myself when I find that I have crossed over to his side of the courtroom. Just the other day an argument began in group about who was the fattest one of us all.

Karen said, "I feel like I don't belong here, because I am fatter than everyone."

Grace immediately said, "You definitely are not fat. I am the fattest one here."

Everyone's "Ed" started jumping into the conversation: "No, I am the fattest."

Of course, Ed was whispering in my ear that I was truly the fattest of all. He provided evidence to prove that fact. He was very convincing. Just before I shouted above everyone else that I was definitely the fattest, I stopped and realized that I would only be defending Ed by saying that.

So, instead, I said to everyone, "This conversation is really uncomfortable for me. It enhances my eating disorder and gets Ed really excited. In fact, I don't think this is a good thing for any of us to be talking about."

All of the Eds in the room let out a big groan. I certainly spoiled all of their fun. There is nothing worse than a fight among girls with eating disorders over who is the fattest. No matter what, Ed always wins that battle.

So we started talking about our insides instead of our outsides and the discussion became a lot more meaningful and helpful to everyone (except to Ed, of course).

I'm Mistaken

"I CAN'T BELIEVE you did that. What were you thinking? How could you make such a stupid mistake at work?" Ms. Perfectionist goes on and on. Occasionally, she throws in her favorite line: "You're such an idiot."

But Ms. Perfectionist is not responsible for all of the airplay in my head. No, Ed is chiming in right along with her. When I make any sort of simple mistake, Ed can go either way regarding what I should do to cope with Ms. Perfectionist's comments about that mistake. Sometimes Ed calls for an all-out binge and purge. "Because you forgot to mail in your rent check this month," Ed says, "you better head to the grocery store and fill up on your favorite binge foods." (It's funny how he never suggests that I should just simply mail in my rent check.) Sometimes he tells me to deal with a mistake by not eating at all. If I forget about an appointment, Ed may say, "Oops, you can't eat today."

Recently, I made a mistake at work that called for starvation. "If you don't eat dinner," Ed said, "you will be able to put Ms. Perfectionist out of your mind, and you will feel better." He continued, "If you don't eat, you will prove that you are powerful and in control—regardless of whatever error you made at work." While Ed made his case about why I shouldn't eat, I decided what I would make for dinner. Ed told me how good it would feel to go to bed on an empty stomach, and I cooked dinner. He insisted that everything would be fine if I just didn't eat. And I ate dinner.

It used to be that when Ed and Ms. Perfectionist teamed up, I had no chance. Ms. Perfectionist would start beating me down, and Ed would jump in for the rescue. For instance, in college, if I missed a question on an exam, Ms. Perfectionist would start in on her belittling comments. To save me from Ms. Perfectionist, Ed would throw out a lifeline. "Just grab this life preserver," he would say, "and I'll pull you safely to shore." In reality, what he said sounded more like, "Just grab all of the food that you can, and you won't have to worry about how you are far less than perfect." Before recovery, I would quickly take Ed's hand and feel momentary relief from Ms. Perfectionist. They sure made a great team.

Today, regardless of what voices are playing in my head, I am able to clearly distinguish Ed's voice from the rest. And I always deal with his voice separately. In other words, I don't let Ms. Perfectionist confuse me about what I know when it comes to Ed. Separating from Ed will work in spite of what Ms. Perfectionist may be screaming in my ear. So, I ignore Ms. Perfectionist, and I handle Ed in the way that I know how. Sure, after I disagree with and disobey Ed, I often still hear Ms. Perfectionist, the Should Monster, or someone else telling me what I should feel. And I am much better equipped to deal with these negative messages when I am in recovery and taking care of myself. Ed can't depend on his friends to help him out anymore, and they can't rely on him for support either. I have severed the ties that once had extreme power over my life, and that's no mistake.

Super Ed

It's a bird. It's a plane. It's Super Ed! Ed always runs to the rescue. Within seconds of having a very minor collision in a parking garage, Ed jumped in with a grand solution. No, he didn't suggest that I simply repaint the small scratches on my bumper. Ed called for an all-out binge. He said, "Wendy's and Taco Bell are just around the corner. You'll need to skip group tonight, so you'll have enough time to really make the binge worth it. Of course, then you'll need to starve yourself for the next two days. That should solve this little car problem." And—silly me—I was actually thinking that I could just buy some touch-up paint and a paintbrush.

Fortunately, I was in the frame of mind to refuse Ed's advice. I did not binge, and I went to group therapy. Furthermore, I followed my entire food plan the next day. In group therapy, I realized just how quickly Ed had entered my mind with a coping mechanism for a few scratches on my car. Nonetheless, I was equally fast in my response: "No!"

Does Ed realize just how completely illogical he is? He actually believes that food is the solution to every problem. When Ed and I were closely intertwined, I followed his advice that promised temporary relief and long-term agony. A fight with my parents called for starvation. If I did less than perfect on an exam in college, he pushed me to binge. I now know that bingeing or starving is never the answer and definitely won't fix scratches on my car.

The fender bender incident occurred at a point when I was very strong in my recovery. It still surprises me today when I hear Ed's voice on extremely good days. He should know that I am just going to listen and then laugh. If I ever do decide that I need the guidance of a complete idiot, it is great to know that Ed will always be there for me.

Faithful to Ed

W HEN I WAS married to Ed, I was a faithful wife. There were no other men in my heart. I had room only for Ed. Even when I did try to include another man in my life, I was far from actually being present in that relationship. For example, I used Ed as a buffer in my relationship with my ex-boyfriend, Brett. With the exception of work, Brett didn't want me to do anything without him. I dealt with my anger about his jealous and controlling nature by pushing Ed front and center in my life. Maybe Brett could control my daily activities, but he could not control what I ate. I tried to starve my anger away. When I didn't eat, I couldn't feel anything. And sometimes I stuffed my anger deep inside myself by bingeing. I specifically remember times when Brett would upset me, and as soon as I had the opportunity, I would walk directly to the kitchen. To the outside world, I was in a relationship with Brett. But inside, it was really just Ed and me. As long as Ed was my focus, I didn't really have to deal with dating and relationships.

Today I am far along in my recovery. And now I am learning about all of those things that I never dealt with before. And it really scares me. I just recently started dating a guy named Scott. Ed is jealous and wants me back as his lovely, devoted wife. In order to convince me to go back with him, Ed says, "Jenni, if you come back to me, you can avoid having to deal with this relationship with Scott. With me in your life, you won't have to think about all of those things that come along with a relationship like feelings and sexuality. Come on and give me another chance." On the day of my first date with Scott, Ed tried to win my heart by suggesting that I binge prior to Scott's arrival at my doorstep. Because I was a little bit nervous about the date that night, I binged. I was back with Ed, and he temporarily numbed my anxiety. Once I even took Ed's advice and actually canceled a date with Scott in order to spend an entire evening with Ed. Who wants to go out and have fun with someone you like when you can wallow in misery at home with someone you hate? Right?

As I continue to date Scott, Ed is really trying hard to get me back. Lately, he does not pass up a chance to say how fat I have become. When Scott opens the door to a restaurant for me on a date, and I walk in ahead of him, Ed says, "Right now, Scott is looking at your fat butt and wondering why he asked you out in the first place. You can't possibly think that you are actually going to eat at this restaurant. What you need to do is refuse to order anything just like you did on your date with Jay two years ago."

Sure, at the time of my first few dates with Scott, Ed charmed me and won me over. But I quickly became aware of what Ed was doing—trying to keep me out of my life again. Now, I am aware of Ed's tactics, and I know that I have a choice of whether or not to act on his comments. Ed still whispers sweet nothings in my ear along the lines of, "Your thighs are like tree trunks" and, "Your stomach reminds me of the Goodyear blimp." I take Ed's comment about as seriously as I take the guy in the bar on a Saturday night who tries the pickup lines: "You must be tired, because you have been running through my mind all night long," "You must be an angel from heaven, because your body is out of this world," or "I lost my phone number, so can I have yours?" With Ed, I just do what I would do with the guy in the bar: I recognize the line as something that doesn't deserve my attention, I turn around, and I walk away.

Tattletale

I N ELEMENTARY SCHOOL, my teachers never had to write my name on the board for being a tattletale. Today, my name is not only on the board but there are many checks behind it. This is because I have learned an appropriate use for tattling. In order to move forward in recovery, we must tell on ourselves to our therapists, doctors, dietitians, and other members of our support team.

During my first two years in recovery, I frequently did not follow the food plan designed by Susan. Instead, I took Ed's advice. His instructions were always revealed in the food journal that I filled out for Susan each week. A typical food chart would have big Xs written under the headings "Monday" and "Tuesday." Under "Wednesday," the single word *binge* would indicate that I had eaten everything in the house and possibly everything within driving range. I never misrepresented any of my meals in my food journal. I was paying my dietitian to help me, and I knew that she could not do that if I was lying. Through rigorous honesty, the bingeing, purging, and starving gradually decreased until I stopped practicing those behaviors.

In addition to being honest with Susan, I have always been 100 percent truthful with Thom. If I relapsed, he was always the first to know. If I refused to listen to him following a relapse, I let him know that, too. On many occasions, I was tempted to simply e-mail Thom and tell him that I was doing fine when I wasn't. But in the end, I would tell him the truth. And Thom was always able to meet me where I was and truly help me.

I have learned that sharing what is going on between Ed and me only serves to benefit me. No one—except Ms. Perfectionist—looks down on me for making mistakes or for falling back into old patterns. Instead, people always offer support and encouragement to keep me moving along the recovery path.

I realize that by tattling I am not obeying my elementary school teachers. They also told me never to begin a sentence with "and" or "but." But some rules are meant to be broken.

Guilty Poster

WHO WOULD COVER up a perfectly good poster of rock star Jon Bon Jovi with stickers of all shapes and sizes? Answer: me.

I admit it. I am guilty. And that is exactly why Bon Jovi got covered with stickers in the first place. Because I felt guilty. It was my "guilty" poster. To the naked eye, it was just a poster covered with gold stars, happy faces, and scratch-and-sniff stickers. But to me, it was a poster that marked progress in my recovery.

Let me explain. There was a time when "I feel guilty" was my mantra. Thom asked me one day if I might have mistaken "I feel guilty" for a punctuation mark.

"What are you talking about?" I asked.

"You just seem to put it at the end of every sentence," he said.

Guess what I felt in that moment?

In that session, I learned about "positive guilt," a term originated, I believe, by Thom's wife, who is also a therapist. Positive guilt is the sense of shame that we feel when we are stepping outside the bounds of what is familiar, when we are breaking the old rules—Ed's rules. Positive guilt is guilt we feel when we are breaking rules that need to be broken.

"It's like withdrawal to a drug addict," Thom explained. "Positive guilt screams at you to turn back, tells you not to dare think for yourself. Positive guilt is the prison guard in the tower shooting you as you sprint for the wall."

So I developed a system for recognizing and even celebrating my positive guilt. I earned stickers for feeling guilty, because for me, feeling guilty meant that I was taking care of myself. It meant that I had finally added my name to the list of people whom I tried to take care of in my life. (Later I learned that I do not have to take care of everyone else anyway.) I felt guilty for eating three meals a day and for spending time focusing on myself in therapy sessions. I felt guilty as I learned to say "no" when that was precisely what I needed to do. And every time I felt guilty, I rewarded myself with a sticker on my guilty poster.

It filled up quickly. At first, Jon Bon Jovi just had scratch-and-sniff strawberry stickers for ears. Then, his eyes became gold stars. (I must admit that he lost some of his sex appeal at this point.) He finally disappeared in an array of colors. Eventually, as I began to not feel guilty about as many things, I stopped earning so many stickers.

But not before I ruined a few good posters.

Guilty-Weird-Amazing

"It's weird," I told Thom.

"What's weird?" he asked.

"Everything. I've had a weird week. First of all, I am not feeling guilty all of the time for everything that I do. I actually told someone 'no' this week without feeling guilty. I have even been following my food plan without feeling guilty. It feels really weird to not feel guilty."

Thom just nodded as therapists do when they think you are onto something. So I kept talking, "I even told a coworker about my eating disorder without worrying what she would think about me. That felt really strange."

When I finished talking, Thom did not say anything but stood up and left the room. He had never done that before when I was in the middle of something that I thought was rather important. "That's weird," I thought to myself.

He walked back into the room and handed me his book, *The Self-Forgiveness Handbook*, opened to a particular page and asked me to read it. The first words I saw on the page read, "Welcoming the Weird." I continued to read a story about a girl actually named Jenny who had gone through a similarly weird week. And apparently the adjective *weird* was not reserved only for Thom's clients named Jennifer. Because in the book, he mentioned that his clients frequently use the words *weird*, *strange*, or *foreign* to describe their lives when they begin to apply what they have been learning in therapy.

That is just what I had been doing. I was finally starting to take what I had learned in therapy and use it in my everyday life. I was beginning to separate from Ed and truly take care of myself. I was treating myself with a new respect and really looking out for my best interest. I was doing the things that I never thought would be possible for me. And that felt really weird.

Moving into this foreign territory was also scary. I found myself in a world where I did not know what was going to happen next, because my responses to what used to be "normal" situations were all different. I began to interact with people in new ways, and I worried about how people would react. I was afraid that I would not be accepted. I was scared to rock the boat.

But that is just what I did. I really jumped up and down all over that boat. And it actually became kind of fun hanging out in uncharted waters. As my new behaviors became a part of my every-day life, I felt less weird each and every day. Actually, I started to feel pretty amazing. In fact, that was my new punctuation mark in therapy sessions. I would end my sentences with, "It's amazing." Eating three meals a day made my body feel amazing. Being able to say "no" to someone when I needed to felt amazing.

I learned in therapy that I had passed through three distinct phases in my recovery. First, I had experienced the "feeling guilty" phase. Then the "weird" portion of my recovery slowly began, which led me to my favorite part, "amazing." I call it my Guilty-Weird-Amazing progression.

You might find yourself somewhere in this very same process. Or you might discover that you pass through another phase that I did not experience. Regardless of what particular stages you go through in your recovery, it is important to keep moving forward. If I had stopped when I reached the guilty or weird phases, I never would have gotten to the amazing life that I experience today. If you keep walking, you, too, will reach a point that feels amazing. You may choose to call this part wonderful, fantastic, or some other variety of amazing. But don't call it unbelievable. Believe it.

Leaving It All up to Ed

H OW MANY TIMES in my life have I turned the power of decision over to Ed? How many times have I been so anxious or
afraid to make a decision that I let Ed decide for me? Unfortunately, the answer is too many to count.

In fact, just today, I was overwhelmed with what I should do
about Scott. We were possibly going to go out tonight, depending
on whether or not I got back from a trip today and depending on
whether or not I actually picked up the phone and called him.
Instead of just looking at this situation as simply whether or not to
call Scott, Ms. Perfectionist jumped in with lots to say.

She said, "Jenni, if you call him, he will think that you want to
see him all of the time, and you will end up in an obsessive,
unhealthy relationship like you had with your last boyfriend."

Ms. Perfectionist didn't stop there: "Jenni, you should not be
dating anyone anyway. You don't have time to waste on that. He'll
just want to marry you, you'll forget about your dreams, and your
life will be completely over."

Ms. Perfectionist successfully overwhelmed me. She trans-
formed the question about calling Scott into a dramatic decision
that would likely determine the course of my life. That is when I
called out for Ed.

"Ed, I really can't handle this situation. Can you take it from
here?"

Ed replied, "Sure, Jenni, don't worry about a thing."

It is important to remember here that the original question was,
"Will Jenni call Scott?" Ed's answer to this particular question was,
"Binge." I'm not quite sure how the question and answer relate to

one another, but Ed always has a way of involving food with every situation.

Ed continued: "You will binge. Then, you will be too tired and sick to go out tonight. Plus, the last thing you will want to do after bingeing is go to a restaurant and eat. All you will want to do is starve for days."

So, I listened to Ed and binged. The decision was made—I will not be going out tonight, so I will not call Scott today.

Hours later, I am sitting here wondering why I let Ed control this aspect of my life—or any aspect for that matter. And I'm wondering, "What can I do right this very moment to take back the power that I gave Ed earlier?" Even though Ed thinks that the decision has been made, I can reopen the question and decide for myself about what I want to do. And my answer is that I want to have fun tonight. So, I am going to call Scott. Ed is throwing a huge fit right now. And Ms. Perfectionist is once again telling me how I will be an unhappy, unsuccessful married woman in less than a year. To both of them, I just want to say, "Chill out. All I am doing is picking up the phone and dialing. No big deal." I'll just take this whole thing one step at a time.

Compare and Despair

Have you ever felt as if there were a Thin Person Convention in town? No matter where you look—the lady in front of you in the grocery store line, the guy crossing the street at Fifth and Broadway, the woman pumping gas at the corner market—everyone is thinner than you. Not only were you not aware that this convention was taking place, but you know that your invitation was not just lost in the mail. You know that you were not invited, and all of a sudden, you see the world through a whole new set of eyes.

On days like this, I think of a phrase that I learned in therapy: "Compare and despair." The fact is that when it comes to body image, I know that I cannot see straight—my vision is literally distorted. So comparing myself to anyone else is just setting myself up for disappointment. There are some days when, regardless of who enters the room and their size, I am going to think that they are thinner than I am. On days when it seems like the thin people are invading, I just think, "Compare and despair," and I shift my focus from them to me.

This simple phrase has been integrated into other areas of my life, too. Now, whenever my town hosts conventions for the National Smart Persons League or the Society of Beautiful Women, I think of those two little words. My happiness no longer depends on the characteristics of those around me. "Compare and despair" has opened my eyes to a new world in which I am free.

I think Ed has a Facebook account, and he loves using it to compare. So, do your best to remember "compare and despair" when online. And don't forget to block triggering people and ads.

Top Ten

I USED TO THINK that a little disc jockey sat in my head and played the Top Ten over and over again. But instead of musical hits, this radio station repeatedly played negative messages about myself. Living with an active eating disorder meant constant self-criticism. Here is the Top Ten playlist that I used to hear all of the time:

1. You are too old.
2. You are lazy.
3. You are selfish for trying to take care of yourself.
4. You are not talented enough.
5. You should/should not have done that.
6. You will never recover.
7. You are not good enough.
8. There is not enough time.
9. You cannot and will not succeed.
10. You do not deserve to be happy.

One day in therapy, I told Thom about the D.J. in my head. Thom thought for a second, and then he asked me, "Are you ready to get those negative messages out of your head?"

"Of course," I said.

"Imagine that those negative messages are being played on a cassette tape in your mind," Thom said.

Immediately, I asked, "Why a cassette tape? It's the twenty-first century. Don't you mean a CD?"

"No," Thom said as he walked across the room and pulled an old cassette tape out of his desk drawer.

He continued, "For this exercise, you need to think of a cassette tape. Imagine that those top ten negative messages are recorded onto this cassette. Imagine that this tape is being played in your mind over and over again. I believe it is called an endless loop tape. Does that feel about right?"

"Yes, that feels perfect," I said, "But I still don't understand why I can't think of a CD."

"Jenni," Thom said, "Stop thinking so much and just stay with me."

He held up the cassette tape and said, "The thoughts that occupy the most time in your head take up a longer length of tape than the ones that only creep in every once in awhile."

He then ripped a piece of tape from the cassette. He gave it to me and asked, "Which negative message is this one?"

Due to the rather long length of this piece of tape, I said, " 'You are lazy.' I sure hear that one a lot."

Thom handed me the cassette tape and said that it was my turn. He encouraged me to pull out a piece of tape for each negative message in my head. As I pulled out each length of tape and told him which negative message it represented, he wrote each particular message on one of ten separate envelopes. He put each piece of tape in its respective envelope. In a matter of minutes, I had symbolically removed the negative messages from my mind. I left Thom's office that day with those top ten negative thoughts taking up space in the envelopes in my backpack instead of my head.

Today when one of the negative tapes begins to play in my head, I just take out the envelope containing that particular thought. I remember that I already removed that thought from my head, and I let the thought pass through freely and leave my mind. Sometimes I realize that I still have a significant piece of a particular negative message playing in my head. When this happens, I just tear another length of tape from the cassette and put it into the appropriate envelope. Now I know why Thom wanted me to take that old, useless cassette tape home with me.

I also know why he insisted that I imagine a cassette tape for this exercise. He didn't want me to smash up any of his CDs. I don't think he trusts me with a hammer.

Too Recovered

Is THERE SUCH a thing as being too recovered? Can you get to a point where you just can't use any more therapy? Can you be "too healthy" to participate in a group therapy session? I used to think so.

I thought, "I don't need to see Thom. I've been following my food plan for three months now," or I asked myself, "Why do I need to go to group tonight? I haven't binged and purged in two weeks." I said, "There's no point in seeing my internist anymore. I have already reached a healthy weight."

I used to think all of these things until I was proved wrong today. As I drove to my therapy session a few hours ago, I thought, "I don't have anything to talk about with Thom today. I'm eating right, and I feel better than ever." Then, Thom and I started talking, and he asked me one question that really stirred my emotions. He asked me why I never went to dinner with the girls after group therapy on Monday nights. It was a very simple question, but it catapulted me back into my fight against workaholism. How can I take the time to enjoy a meal with friends when there is always so much work waiting for me to get done at home?

At the end of the therapy session, I was a little discouraged and said to Thom, "I came into this session actually thinking that I was going to bore you with my lack of personal problems. Now, I'm leaving feeling as if I have so much more work to do. And I had thought that I was doing so well in my recovery."

Thom reassured me by saying, "Just because you have work to do does not mean that you are regressing. You haven't lost any of the progress that you have made in your recovery. You have simply come to the realization that you have a lot more work to do. Remember that we are always a work in progress."

Does this mean that we have to be in therapy for the rest of our lives? Does it mean that we can never miss another group session? I'm not saying either of these things. All that I am saying is that in my experience, you can always benefit from digging deep inside and getting to know yourself better. Now, when I start thinking that I am "too recovered" for this or that, I will challenge myself to really open my mind and even stretch my limits. For instance, in my next group session, I will talk about that seemingly simple question that Thom asked me today. I have always heard that you can never be too rich. (I must admit that I don't have any experience in this area.) But I will say you can never be too recovered.

When Will He Stop?

WHEN WILL ED stop trying to control me? When will Ed just go away and leave me alone? These were questions that I asked the health care professionals on my support team. They all said, "Maybe never." They actually looked me in the eyes and told me that Ed might never stop trying to run my life.

Well, this was not an acceptable answer to me. "Why am I even doing this whole recovery thing if Ed is never going to go away?" I asked. "Why do I bother fighting him if he is just going to win in the end?"

This is where I was wrong. It took me a while to realize that Ed's persistent pestering does not guarantee his victory. No matter how long Ed tries to control me, I still win if I disagree with and disobey him. I still win if I decide to take care of myself in spite of Ed's constant criticisms and maneuvers to control me.

Even now I hear Ed's voice. The difference today is that I do not follow Ed's instructions anymore. He throws out his comments about what I should and should not do, and I continue living my life the way I want to—my way—the way that is best for me.

In ten years, will Ed still come around? I have no idea. Maybe he won't. Maybe I will not hear his voice at all. Or maybe he will just come around on special occasions—like Thanksgiving or other holidays where food is the focus. I cannot predict the future. It would be nice to think that Ed might just disappear, but it is even better to know that he does not have to go anywhere in order for me to live a fulfilled and happy life.

Thom's Turn

1. Define Your Recovery

We are seldom at a loss to describe what is wrong or bad in our lives or what it is like to be stuck. But we are often at a complete loss to describe what we want instead. It is important to be able to identify and describe something about what you want for yourself—if you intend to find it, that is. Can you define your recovery? Do you know what you have in mind when you think about recovering from your eating disorder? Not what your mother or father or brother or sister or therapist or dietitian think your recovery should be. Do you know what *you* want it to be?

Try this simple exercise to begin formulating your personal goals in recovery. Characterize your recovery at each of these four levels: spiritual (sense of purpose, connection, and meaning), mental (what you are thinking), emotional (what you are feeling), and physical (what you are doing with food and with exercise). Be as specific as possible. And remember: this is your personal definition for your recovery.

When I am in recovery from my eating disorder . . .

Spiritually, I _____

Mentally, I _____

Emotionally, I _____

Physically, I _____

2. Negative Thoughts

Eating disorders are characterized by constant self-criticism. Do negative messages constantly run through your head? Write down your top-ten negative thoughts. If you can find an old cassette tape, you might want to try the exercise that Jenni did in the section titled, "Top Ten."

Now here's the challenge. For each of your negative thoughts, write a corresponding alternative thought that you would like to hear instead. If your negative thought is "I hate myself," a corresponding thought might be, "I love myself." Or it might be more realistic for your corresponding thought to be "I love some things about myself," or "I'm learning to love myself."

The next time a negative thought enters your mind, try to remember the alternative thought and repeat it to yourself. More than likely, coming up with the negative thoughts will be much easier than the alternatives. Be patient with yourself. Start a list of positive alternative thoughts in your journal and build on it. When you become aware of negative self-talk, use that awareness as an opportunity to work on your list of alternatives.

This is hard work, but well worth the effort.

3. Writing Dialogue with Ed

I told you about how Jenni sometimes sends me her daily food plans via e-mail. That is not the only way that Jenni and I use e-mail as a part of her therapy. Periodically, Jenni also e-mails me dialogue between Ed and herself. In the subject line of these e-mails, she types "Ed/Jenni Dialogue." When I see that subject line among all of the messages in my in-box, I know that Jenni has been confronting Ed in her life. Jenni finds that actually writing out dialogue with Ed helps her to connect better with herself and to fight harder against Ed. Here is an example of an actual e-mail that Jenni sent to me:

ED: You are so fat, especially your stomach. You need to start starving.

JENNI: Once again, you are telling me that I am fat. This is no secret, Ed. I already know that YOU think I'm fat. Tell me something that I don't know.

ED: You are fat. I just want you to accept it.

JENNI: Ed, you play tricks with my eyes. I know that I don't see my body correctly. You are the only person in my life who has ever told me that I was fat. You are wrong!

ED: (doesn't know what to say)

By writing out dialogue over and over again, Jenni actually learned how to stump Ed. That, however, is not the goal. The purpose of this exercise is merely to help you separate from Ed. Whether you agree with Ed or not, it is important to practice this separation.

Try writing out what Ed says to you and how you respond. Like Jenni, you might even find it helpful to share this dialogue with someone on your support team.

Related to the "Top Ten" section earlier and exercise 2 in this section, many find it beneficial to keep a playlist of inspirational songs on their smartphones or MP3 players. Because music was so powerful in my own healing, I've included a song that I co-wrote, also called "Life Without Ed," at the end of this book. Further, you might want to play the audio book for *Life Without Ed*, and other positive books, in your car or at home—to combat Ed's nonstop negative voice.

5

ED'S LAST STAND

Surviving Relapse

Relapse is inevitable. It will happen. Relapse is a normal and even necessary part of recovery. I made a point to learn something from each relapse, and I grew stronger and stronger. I had many relapses, and I am still not perfect today. Ed will not let you walk away easily. But no matter how hard he fights, you *can* walk away. When he blocks you, step around him and keep moving. Part 5 will show you how.

My Invisible Child

"YOU ARE FAT. You are fat. You are fat. Did I mention that you are fat?"

This is what Ed says to me these days. And after all of my hard work in recovery, there is actually something inside me that still believes him. Who am I kidding? There is something inside me that just won't let go, something inside me that is clinging to Ed with a death grip, something that has chained itself to Ed with a heavy-duty lock and thrown away the key. There is something inside me that wants Ed that much.

It makes me wonder what that little part sees in Ed. Does Ed possibly have some redeeming qualities? First and foremost, Ed assures me that as long as I stay with him I will never get fat. And if I never get fat, I will never be a failure. Second, with Ed, I am special, unique, different from everyone else. After all, I am the only person in the world with an eating disorder, right? And what about control? Ed keeps my life all tied up in a pretty package with a ribbon on top.

So, I guess that little part inside yearns for Ed's promises. That little part doesn't want to be a failure. It wants to be special. And that little part wants to be in control. How can I convince that part of me that Ed cannot really deliver any of those things?

In therapy, I learned that I do not have to convince that little part of anything. I learned that the part of me that holds onto Ed is the little girl inside. It is the little girl who thought she was fat in dance class at four years old. It is the girl who refused to eat cake at birthday parties in elementary school.

"Do you trust Ed to baby-sit the little girl inside you?" Thom asked one day. "Do you trust him to be with her at all, knowing what you know about him?"

It was one of those therapy moments, what I have come to think of as very busy moments of silence. I had never thought of it this way.

Thom continued, "If you were caring for a little girl—maybe one of your friend's children—how would you feel about Ed being in charge of that child?"

"Horrible," I said.

"Why horrible?" Thom asked.

"Because I know what Ed would be saying to her, how he would be insulting and abusing her. I know that he would either starve her or insist that she gorge herself on massive amounts of food." It was all very clear to me. "No way I would let Ed near her," I said.

So I learned that I need to treat this little girl as I would a child who has fallen under the influence of Ed. I didn't need to convince her of anything; I needed to accept responsibility for taking good care of her. I didn't need to tell her that she was doing something wrong; I needed to do something right. I was scared, but I began to accept responsibility for parenting my invisible child.

During a therapy session, I did a role-play with the little girl within me. The conversation went like this:

JENNI: Why do you hold onto Ed?

INVISIBLE CHILD: He takes care of me. I'm scared to be without him.

JENNI: Ed just lies to you over and over again. From now on, I would like to be the one who takes care of you. I love you.

INVISIBLE CHILD: I don't trust you.

JENNI: I know you don't, and for good reason. I have left you with Ed in the past, but that is changing. I will be taking care of you now, and that includes protecting you from Ed. I want you to learn to trust me.

INVISIBLE CHILD: I will try to trust you, but it won't be easy. I still trust Ed.

JENNI: I know you do. For now just know that I am always here for you—even when you are holding hands with Ed.

Now, when I find something inside me that won't let go of Ed, I know what it is—I know who it is. She is the little girl inside. I ask her what she needs from me. I tell her that I can provide her with all of those things that Ed only promises.

Caring for my invisible child teaches me about self-compassion. It helps me not to beat myself up when I have setbacks with Ed. After all, I would never beat up on a little child—real or invisible.

Do you have an invisible child inside of you? Maybe you can't see this child, but I'll bet if you listen carefully, you can hear what that tender voice is saying. Close your eyes. Breathe. Sit quietly. And listen.

If you connect with this section as well as the "Baby Pictures" exercise in part 3 (on page 85), try this: set a childhood photo of yourself as the background image on your mobile phone. This can serve as a reminder to practice greater self-compassion. Take this a step further and set the same childhood photo as the profile image for those who call you the most. Then, each call from these people can be a self-love reminder!

Relapse

ONE YEAR. I had one solid year of recovery under my belt (intended or not, the pun is obvious). I had not been under the influence of Ed for one entire year. Then, one afternoon when I was driving home from work, out of nowhere, Ed appeared, put both of his hands on the steering wheel, and took control. Normally, I cannot stand backseat drivers, and I quickly make it clear that I don't need their help. Now, I actually had a front-seat driver, and I said nothing. Absolutely nothing.

It did not take me long to realize that Ed was headed to our old hangout—the golden arches. And I knew that he was not just interested in playing on the playground this time. No, he was ready to do some serious super-sizing. As we were sitting in the drive-through line, my cell phone rang. I recognized the phone number as belonging to Lynne, a girl from group therapy. What perfect timing. I was on the verge of relapse, and Lynne called to save me. It was as if a police officer had walked into a bank while it was getting robbed. But unlike the bank teller, I did not scream for help. No, I let Ed answer the phone. He proceeded to tell Lynne how everything was wonderful and that nothing could be better. Of course, he did not identify himself as Ed and pretended to be me. He said good-bye to Lynne as he grabbed the large bag of food from the lady at the drive-through window, and we were on our way—to relapse.

Even though I had not binged, purged, or starved for a year, the old behaviors came right back to me. I was surprised that the behaviors were even worse than when I had given them up. I spent days feeling bad about having relapsed, and I continued to follow Ed's instructions.

Several days after my outing with Ed, I was sitting in group listening to the conversations going on around me. I was not participating, because I was still enjoying Ed's company too much to want to say anything about it. Furthermore, Ms. Perfectionist did not want me to admit to everyone that my recovery was not perfect. Even when I am not particularly talkative in group, I always keep my ears open and am often amazed by what I hear. On this day, I overheard Lori and Dawn talking:

Lori: Yeah, I just relapsed yesterday.

Dawn: But you're getting yourself back on track, right?

Lori: Well, um, not exactly.

Dawn: Why not? You should treat your relapse just like a leak in your roof.

Lori: I have no idea what you're talking about.

Dawn: A relapse is just like a leaky roof. When you have one, you have to do something about it immediately. Sitting around feeling bad about it won't do you a bit of good.

It makes sense. A relapse is like a leak in the roof. We do not plan for it. Sometimes we do not know why it started. But we must take care of it as soon as possible. We must make it a priority. Just think about it. If water were dripping steadily from your ceiling onto your leather sofa, you would not sit down and wallow in sadness for a while over the fact that your sofa was getting ruined. No, you would take action quickly. Move the sofa; patch the roof. And that is just what has to be done with relapse.

As soon as I realized that a quick reaction time was the key to overcoming a relapse, I started to get back on track. I called my support team. I disobeyed Ed. I started to eat right, and I felt great again. Sure, since that day Ed took me to McDonald's, I have had other bad days here and there. But I'm not complaining. I used to have bad years.

Now there is a note taped to my bathroom mirror that says simply, "Move the sofa; patch the roof."

The Next Right Thing

E D BLINDSIDED ME. After several months of following my
food plan with no bingeing and purging, yesterday, Ed came
on strong with wanting me to binge. The situation was perfect for
him. I was extremely hungry. I was at a place where I had frequently binged before. And I was bored. So, Ed took the opportunity to say, "Jenni, I know exactly what to do here. It will be
fun—for old times' sake." Before I even knew it was happening,
Ed had me. I was in the middle of a binge. Then, Ed really jumped
in stronger. He said, "Well, I guess you're back with me now. And
you actually thought you were 'recovered.' Of course, tomorrow
you are going to have to starve all day long in order to make up for
this binge. Then, you'll need to restrict all week."

"No," I said to myself. "I will not go back there." The day after
the binge, I refused to go back to Ed. Just that one night with him
reminded me of how miserable I was with him—how trapped I
was. Instead I followed the advice that someone gave a girl in group
therapy not long ago after she had relapsed. The advice was, "Do
the next right thing." For that girl, the next right thing was to go
home after group and eat dinner. For me, the next right thing was
to eat breakfast.

Eating breakfast would be a huge violation of Ed's rules. He
says, "If you eat breakfast, you won't be able to fit into that dress
to wear to the baby shower today. If you eat breakfast, forget about
ever wearing those jeans that you just bought. If you eat breakfast,
you're going to have to work out extra hard this week. If you eat
breakfast, you're a failure." I'll admit it. At the time, I almost agreed
with Ed. He is very convincing. But, even if I agreed with Ed, I
could still disobey him, which is what I did.

Food is something I am going to have to face at least three times a day for the rest of my life. And I am not perfect. But one really bad day does not mean that I am hopeless and back at square one with my eating disorder. Olympic ice skaters fall in their quest for the gold. Heisman Trophy winners throw interceptions. Professional singers forget the words. And people with eating disorders sometimes slip back into an old pattern. But all of these individuals just pick themselves back up and do the next right thing. The ice skater makes the next jump. The football player throws the next pass. The singer finishes the song. And I am going to eat breakfast.

Pick up the Phone

WHY DIDN'T I just call someone today? Why didn't I call one of the many people on my support team? It's easy. Pick up the phone and dial. But I didn't do it, and what happened? As always when I don't call someone, I relapse. And now I feel miserable and depressed.

It is a proven fact that if I call someone when I am on the verge of giving in to Ed, I will not relapse. Instead, I have a conversation with someone on my support team, and by the time I hang up the phone, I don't want to binge, purge, or starve. Even if Ed is still tempting me, I am stronger with the renewed energy I need to tell him no.

But this time I did not call someone when I started to feel as if my eating disorder was taking control of my day. The only thing I could think about was eating more and more food. I wanted to binge and numb myself of feelings of anxiety and restlessness. I should have called someone for support. I was feeling very weak. I definitely needed support—support I could have easily received by simply picking up the phone. I always have everyone's phone numbers with me, everywhere I go. I had the numbers, but I didn't even attempt to connect. And I relapsed.

Looking back, I realize why I did not call someone. When I first started having eating disordered thoughts, I did not stop and separate myself from Ed. I immediately let him possess my body and mind and make all of the decisions. With Ed in control, calling for support was not an option.

The next time I start having Ed thoughts, I need to slow down and breathe. I need to remember what happens when I act too quickly and fail to separate myself from Ed. I need to remember that Ed makes me feel extremely agitated and out of control. The most important thing that I need to do next time is separate myself from Ed, determine what I think, and listen for what Ed is saying. It might sound something like this:

ED: Jenni, skip lunch today. You're too busy at work to eat today.

JENNI: Ed, I know what you are doing. You just want to take over my life again. I'm going to call someone for support right now.

ED: You don't have time to call anyone. Look at that big pile of work on your desk.

JENNI: If I don't call someone, I will end up going back to you. Then, I really won't be able to get any work done. All I will be able to think about is food and weight.

ED: I won't completely take over your life this time. All I want you to do is skip one little meal.

JENNI: I'm picking up the phone right now.

I wish this scenario had happened today, but it did not. I wish that I would have called someone prior to my relapse. My hope is that you can learn from my mistake. Always have the phone numbers of people on your support team with you, everywhere you go. And most important, call them. If no one answers the phone on your first attempt to reach out, start over and call everyone again. If no one answers, leave messages. Even talking about Ed on a voice message has helped me to find strength when I needed it. Ed has proved many times that he can beat me alone, but when I join with others, I can win. And I do win.

Richard Simmons,
Eat Your Heart Out

RICHARD SIMMONS, eat your heart out. Because here comes Ed. It's not that Ed looks great in a spandex bodysuit or anything, but he does have the persistence required to get someone off of the couch and into the gym for hours at a time. Until now, I never had the desire to exercise compulsively. No, Ed waited for me to experience years in recovery before he pulled out that little trick. He just really doesn't want our divorce to remain final.

I never thought that I could possibly become addicted to exercise, because I dreaded it. I did not look forward to aerobics, the treadmill, or my Cindy Crawford workout video. Exercise was just something that I had to do to stay healthy. I would cross it off my list of things to do and be glad that it was done. But not today.

Today, Ed wants me to use all of my free time to exercise. He even wants me to exercise at work. He makes any excuse for me to get up from my desk and walk around. His theory is that the more I move, the thinner I will become. He urges me to take the long route to the office water cooler to burn extra calories. This route entails weaving in and out of a particular set of cubicles and walking circles around the break room. (And I wonder why my coworkers look at me strangely.) And what about my nervous habit of shaking my leg up and down? I used to do this 40 percent of the time while I was at work. Now, Ed wants me to do it 100 percent of the time. This way I can sit at my desk and still burn calories.

On Monday, Ed almost convinced me to skip group therapy to go to the gym instead—regardless of the fact that I had already attended an aerobics class that same day. And today, after I finished my exercise class, Ed begged me to stay for just one more session. I will admit that I have an addictive personality. If I start giving in to Ed now, I know that I can become a really devoted exercise addict.

So, what am I doing? I am going back to the basics—separating myself from Ed. I am having conversations with him, so I know what he is saying, and I know where I stand. Then, I disagree with and disobey him. And once again—just like in the beginning—it is very difficult not to do what Ed is so cleverly telling me that I need to do. But I am doing just that, one step at a time.

Ed sure gets a lot of use out of his tank top and gym shorts these days. He is standing at every corner—holding my sneakers—encouraging me to exercise. He says, "Jenni, let's go walk on the treadmill for a few hours. Maybe you can trim those thighs down a little bit."

I respond, "You go walk on the treadmill. I am going to meet a friend for coffee."

"It's your choice. You can choose between fat thighs or your friend," Ed says.

"No, Ed. Right now, I am choosing between a prison with you and a life of freedom. I choose freedom today."

I will choose it again tomorrow.

Does Ed have a say in your exercise behaviors? Take the compulsive exercise test at jennischaefer.com/cet. Discuss your results with a qualified health care professional.

Maybe It's Not Too Late

AFTER A LENGTHY separation, when our divorce had been filed, papers served, Ed came back for an extended visit. Maybe, we thought, just maybe, we could still make this relationship work. Maybe it wasn't too late. I am told that lots of divorcing couples go through this "let's give it one more try" kind of thing. Strangely, Thom did not seem to understand. He had been so patient before—far more patient with me than I had been with myself—but now he seemed noticeably impatient, even irritated. I thought that I might know what was bothering him, but I wasn't sure. You see, I was back under the spell of my longtime, controlling, abusive "friend," Ed.

Thom always emphasizes that every moment is an opportunity to begin recovery. If you drop the ball, pick it right back up and keep moving. He told me that my relapse (that's what he called Ed's and my reunion) could end at any moment, that it was my choice. Much like when I had first begun to work with Thom, I could hear him talking, but I wasn't really too sure what he was saying. He seemed to think that I could simply make the choice to get up and walk away from Ed. He just didn't seem to understand. I wondered what had happened to the patient, understanding, and wise therapist. This new version of Thom was beginning to get on my nerves. In response to an e-mail I sent him, Thom wrote, "Do you want me to help you end this relapse today—right now? No is an acceptable answer, so think about it. If you say yes, I want you to agree to follow my instructions without arguing with me." For some reason Thom was thinking that I had become stubborn lately. As I said, I wasn't sure what was wrong with him lately.

I thought about his offer, and to my surprise (Thom told me later that he wasn't surprised), I said no. I turned down his offer to help me get away from Ed. After three years, after lots of hard work, and after amazing success in recovery from my eating disorder, I was right back in it, as if I had never even left. Jenni and Eddie sittin' in a tree, K-I-S-S-I-N-G.

Something finally got my attention. It was how horrible my life had become after only seven days with Ed. Getting back together with him was pure misery, and almost instantly so. I didn't have energy to write or sing; I couldn't think straight at work; and I had no desire to be with any of my friends.

I could feel Ed smirking. "Just like old times," he said.

Ed consumed all of my time and all of my energy. There was nothing left for me or anyone else. Maybe it *was* too late to make it work with Ed. He would never admit it, but try as I might, I could not successfully throw away all of the good recovery that I had experienced.

The next morning I sent Thom an e-mail with a very simple message: "OK. I'm here. Instruct."

The Plastic Bat

THOM HANDS ME a plastic baseball bat, and I start swinging. I am not trying to hit a baseball. No, I am swinging at a much larger and more stationary target—the couch in Thom's office. I am angry at Ed, and I am able to release some of my frustration by beating up on the couch.

I yell at Ed, "I hate you. I don't need you anymore." Other times I do not even say words; I just scream. At first, I am conscious of what the therapist in the office next door might think, but then I loosen up and just let myself go.

When I take a break from hitting his furniture, Thom asks, "How do you feel now?"

I answer, "I feel relieved. I feel free. I feel strong."

My therapy sessions are not always as loud and physically active. Sometimes we sit in silence and just focus on our breaths together.

Thom says, "When you breathe in, focus on pulling positive energy into your body." I breathe slowly and think about bringing joy, happiness, and love into my body.

"When you breathe out," Thom continues, "focus on releasing negative energy." I breathe out and think about depression, hopelessness, and Ed exiting my body.

After only three breaths like this, I feel calm, peaceful, and relaxed. Just three breaths.

Thom has taught me numerous techniques that involve moving energy in my body to help me to deal with difficult feelings. I use these techniques not only in Thom's office; I also bring them home with me. Thom even let me borrow the bat once, so I could use it on my bed. It is amazing how much better I feel after taking a few swings at my mattress. One of my favorite techniques is standing in a doorway and pressing my arms out. Pressing against the resistance of the door frame helps me to release pent-up feelings, especially anger and frustration. Another technique to move energy is to scream into a pillow as loud as I can. This way I get all of my feelings out, and my neighbors don't have to call 911. When the weather is nice, I get up and move my whole body around by walking through the park near my home.

I have discovered that moving energy through my body serves as a great relapse-prevention tool for me. In the same way that picking up the phone and calling someone helps me to avoid relapse, these techniques allow me to deal successfully with feelings that I experience when I am on the verge of relapse. After taking a few swings at the furniture, screaming at the top of my lungs, or just concentrating on my breathing, I usually do not want to binge, purge, or starve as much as I had previously. Moving energy helps bring me to a place where I can confront Ed with strength and confidence.

Ed made his opinion about my energy-moving techniques very clear to me. He said, "You are such an idiot. Why are you yelling at your pillow? Normal people do not hit things and scream like that. Recovery is crazy, and so are you."

At first, I agreed with Ed. When I heard his voice, I would stop whatever I was doing. Often I would turn to his suggestions. Slowly, I was able to trust Thom and let myself try new things. It took a while before I was not uptight, self-conscious, and worried about what other people would think of me. But finally, I reached the point where I was able to really give a piece of furniture a good, solid beating.

Now, when I am moving energy around inside, Ed does not have anything to say. He just stays out of my way.

Don't Figure It Out

IMAGINE THAT YOUR house is burning down around you. A fire-fighter is close by urging you to follow him to safety. Meanwhile, Ed has a tight grip on your arm and is pulling you toward the flames. Ed says, "We need to get a closer look. We need to find out why this fire started. If we just figure it out, we can make sure that it will never happen again." As you get closer and closer to the flames, you feel the heat against your body. The firefighter is at your side and could easily pull you to safety if you would just reach out your hand. But you don't. You are too busy listening to Ed.

This is what I did today. The only difference was that the fire was my relapse. The firefighter was really my support team encouraging me to get back on the road to recovery. And Ed, well, he played himself. Instead of listening to my support team, I followed Ed's advice. I stayed in the middle of my relapse and tried to figure it out. Why had I relapsed? What could I do differently in the future to avoid a similar relapse? What could I do this week to ensure that I stay in recovery? Even Thom admitted that these were great questions to answer—but not while I was sitting in flames. Thom said that before all other things, I first needed to get out of the fire.

I will admit that it was not easy to get out of the burning house today. Ed was making so much sense to me. I really thought that I needed to figure everything out before I started eating right again. I just needed one more day of contemplation. Of course, Ed didn't bother to tell me that by then, I would have been engulfed in flames. Finally, I became willing to at least listen to my support team. In the end, it took three really strong firefighters—Thom, Kristina, Sarah—and a lot of willingness to get me to safety. Now,

I am safe. I am eating right, and I am thinking clearly again. Only now is it the right time for me to sit down and try to answer those questions that I posed earlier. After all, it is only after the fire has been extinguished that investigators go on the scene to begin their work.

In emergency situations, Ed will always tell you to follow his path to safety. In a hurricane, instead of driving you out of town by car, he will suggest that you take a boat. "We really need to get to the eye of the storm," he will say, "so that we know what kind of winds we are dealing with." Ed is the guy who will run straight for a tornado. He is a real-life storm chaser. Don't let him take you along for the ride.

And don't try to figure it out.

Research

I RECENTLY SPENT THREE days in hell. To be less dramatic, I spent three days in relapse. Ed says that I was an angel for those three days. My vocal coach, Judy, says that I spent the three days in the field doing research for this book. She's right. I was back in the depths of my eating disorder again. And when that happens, I always try to learn something new—something that might help other people just like me.

My relapse started one afternoon at work. Out of nowhere, Ed told me that I needed to binge. Instead of separating myself from Ed and disagreeing with him, I immediately obeyed him. "Yes," I said to Ed, "these cookies with the extra layer of fudge and peanut butter are sure to solve all of my problems for the day. And if they don't, these pastries with the cream-filled centers definitely will." After bingeing all afternoon, Ed said, "You might as well cancel your therapy appointment tonight. Just relax and let me guide you through the evening." At that point, I did finally separate from Ed, and I said, "I am going to my appointment, and you can't stop me." And he didn't. I went to my therapy session, and I reported everything that was going on. I even made two support calls from the session. When neither of the girls I called answered, Ed said, "Great! Now, when they call you back tonight, we just won't answer the phone." I responded, "You're right, Ed. 'We' won't answer the phone tonight, but I will."

I stayed connected to my support team not only through phone calls but also through e-mail. I sent out an SOS via e-mail to everyone on my support team. I told them that I was in distress and needed words of encouragement. I even decided that I should attend an additional support group that the girls had started getting together for on Thursday nights. So, I went to group and really found my strength again. In fact, I left the support group with one thing in mind: I was going to eat dinner. All day Ed had been telling me that I needed to starve. Prior to group, I had listened to him. But after group, I knew that I had the strength to disobey him. I went home and ate despite Ed's comments about how fat I would get if I ate dinner at 10:00 at night. I ate, and I went to bed with a whole new freedom.

And I woke up this morning feeling like Jenni again. What got me through this last relapse was staying connected to my support team. At every corner, I had someone telling me that I could do it—that I could fight Ed. People were calling me, e-mailing me, and telling me to my face. I could not get away from all of the support. I didn't want to. It felt so good knowing that people were standing behind me.

In college, I did numerous research reports as I earned my bachelor of science in biochemistry. The most important part of every report was always the conclusion. So, I must conclude this from my most recent research with Ed: if I stay connected to my support team, Ed will not have the strength to push me down. If I do not isolate, Ed will not win. I never have to fight Ed alone. And neither do you.

One Day

ONE DAY. I was back with Ed for only one day, and already my life was crazy and out of control. Not even a full twenty-four hours with Ed led to madness, misery, and hopelessness. And each time I go back with Ed, he is worse. He causes more havoc than ever before. The more time I spend in recovery, the worse each relapse gets. When I relapse now, I absolutely cannot function in my everyday life. I am not able to perform my duties at work. I can't sing or write. The truth is that I just can't afford to lose any more of my life to Ed. I have given him enough. That's why I chose to eat dinner last night.

"Have you eaten dinner yet?" Scott asked me when I arrived at his house yesterday evening. This is a seemingly simple question with only a couple of possible answers. But it sent me into a wave of panic. I thought to myself, "No. I haven't eaten dinner. I'm in the middle of a relapse. And Ed has designated today as a non-eating day."

Just prior to arriving at Scott's house, I had attended a support group. The girls had encouraged me to find my strength and specifically urged me to tell Scott that I really needed to eat dinner.

When I finally answered Scott's question, I said, "Ed won't let me eat today. But the truth is that I really need to eat something. I need to eat dinner right now." I could tell that Ed thought I was bluffing.

"What do you want? I'll fix you something," Scott said.

"It's not that easy, Scott," I said, "Ed tells me that if I eat something today, I am a weak person. If I were strong, I would not eat dinner tonight."

It became obvious to me that Scott does not live by Ed's rules. He clearly didn't know the consequences of eating on a non-eating day. And he quickly corrected me by saying that eating dinner would be an indication of strength, not weakness.

As we talked, I became more and more open to the idea of eating dinner. But something still held me back. Ed told me that everyone including Scott would look down on me if I ate. Ed said that people would look up to me if I did not eat. I explained these thoughts to Scott.

"Why would anyone look down on you for eating? Everyone has to eat. We eat to live," he said.

"Well, I want to live," I said.

So I ate dinner. Ed yelled repeatedly while I was eating: "You are such a failure! You are a loser!" He said that I had ruined my entire day. But deep in my heart I knew that I had just catapulted myself out of a very destructive relapse. I was back on the road to recovery—feeling a bit shaky—but prepared to fight any more battles that might come my way.

No matter how out of control my relapses get, it is nice to know that I can always step right out of them with the same basic recovery principles. I always need to listen for what Ed is telling me to do and then disobey him. Separating from Ed always works—no matter how far along you are in recovery and no matter how far you've fallen into relapse. I don't have to spend another twenty-four hours with Ed. As soon as I realize that Ed is running the show, I can do what I need to do to get back on track in a matter of moments. I won't give Ed one more day. Not one day.

Thom's Turn

1. Emergency 911 Card

One important component of Jenni's recovery has been relapse prevention. She has developed various ways to prevent the onset of a relapse. I encouraged Jenni to make an emergency 911 card that includes relapse-prevention tips. Jenni decided to make the card and carry it with her at all times. On one side of the card, Jenni included a list of phone numbers of people on her support team. The other side of the card included a list of what has really worked in the past in preventing a relapse. Here is one side of Jenni's emergency 911 card:

1. Move energy.
    a. Push arms against resistance. (Stand in a doorway and push arms out.)
    b. Breath in (good energy).
       Breathe out (bad energy).
    c. Punch bed.
    d. Scream into a pillow.
2. Have a conversation with Ed. Separate. Disagree. Disobey.
3. Take a walk.
4. Call people on support team.

Make your own emergency 911 card. You can make it the size of a credit card and carry it in your wallet. Jenni had her card laminated and attached it to her key chain. The important thing is to carry the emergency card with you everywhere you go. Use it when you need it, avoid relapse, and stay on the recovery path.

2. Intervening on a Relapse

Do you predictably relapse in certain situations? Are there certain events that take place prior to each relapse? For instance, Jenni used to relapse around the time of specific stressful events at work. The better you understand the patterns associated with your relapses, the more effectively you will be able to interrupt Ed before a relapse begins.

Use your answers to the following questions to improve your ability to intervene on your relapse patterns:

- What are the most dangerous triggers to relapse for you?
- Do you always relapse when you encounter these triggers? If not, what are some things you have done to avoid relapse in these situations?
- How does a relapse begin for you? Does it begin with a thought? With an emotion? With a physical feeling?
- On a scale of 1 to 10 (10 being very much), how badly do you want to learn to successfully intervene on your relapses?
- What is one thing you are willing to seriously try for interrupting your next potential relapse?
- What are the best questions to ask yourself about relapse?

3. Anti-Ed Device

Similar to the 911 emergency card, Jenni also created what she referred to as her very own anti-Ed device to help her remain strong in the event of a potential relapse. Her anti-Ed device is simple. It is a letter to herself. When Jenni was at a solid place in her recovery, she wrote a letter to herself to be read when she is on the verge of relapsing. I think of it as a sort of time-travel letter. A Jenni strong in her recovery today writes a letter to be delivered to a more vulnerable, struggling Jenni sometime in the undisclosed future.

When Jenni reads the letter, she can be reminded of the horror associated with Ed and offer herself a helping hand. Here is Jenni's letter:

Dear Jenni,
You are feeling so overwhelmed right now. You are feeling completely out of control. The only thing that I want to tell you is: YOU DO HAVE A CHOICE. You do not have to turn to Ed. Yes, I know that in the past, Ed has been your escape from the feelings. And for the moment, Ed seems to work. But in the long run, YOU WILL REGRET GOING TO ED. He makes you depressed and miserable. He makes promises that he never keeps. I just got over a relapse. I wish I had said no to Ed at the first moment that I heard him. YOU CAN DO THAT RIGHT NOW.
Love,
Jenni

Make your very own anti-Ed device. Write a simple letter to yourself. Carry it with you always and read it when you are in danger of relapsing. Revise the letter as your recovery strengthens; as you gain more wisdom in your recovery, include that wisdom in your time-travel letter, your anti-Ed device. Through the letter you can remind yourself of the pain that Ed brings into your life and encourage yourself to stay strong in your recovery.

If you know predictable times ahead when you are vulnerable to relapse (for instance, during the holidays or final exams), send your future self an encouraging e-mail using a website like futureme.org.

6

THE HARD TRUTH

Getting Serious About
Getting Better

To recover from my eating disorder, I had to make a decision to do whatever it takes to change my relationship with Ed, including eating healthfully, attending necessary appointments, and making support calls. I had to be willing to feel the pain that goes along with recovery. It was all worth it in the end. Some parts of recovery will seem impossible to tackle. But I am living, breathing proof that it is possible. Part 6 will help you to make a true commitment to your health and will move you along some of those difficult recovery roads.

Recovery First

I T IS THE NIGHT before the long-awaited big day in the recording studio, and I don't want to binge and purge. Tomorrow, I
will record my voice on a CD to last for all time, and I don't want
to starve. In fact, I have been following my food plan, which means
I will be able to concentrate in the studio. Because I finally put
recovery first in my life—above my singing career—I will be able
to focus on my voice for the recording session.

It used to be the other way around. On my list of priorities,
recovery was barely squeezed in at the very bottom of the page.
What really mattered was written in neatly just beneath "To
Do"—send a birthday card to every person I have ever met in my
entire life, attend every show of every performer in Nashville, and
bake brownies for every special occasion within a thirty-mile
radius of my home. Before I moved recovery above all of these
things, I resented everyone on their birthday, I never listened at
performances, and I did not dare eat a bite of Jenni's Famous
Brownies.

In addition to keeping Hallmark in business, pursuing a music
career was also more important than recovery. Songwriting was a
great excuse for not going to group therapy. I wrote nothing even
close to inspirational on the evenings I chose to skip group. How
could I with Ed constantly throwing out his suggestions? When
cowriting with Ed, I'm surprised that we didn't write a song titled,
"Starving for You," "Don't Eat a Thing," or "Ain't Nothing but a
Corn Dog."

Only when I put recovery first was I finally able to focus on
everything else that I wanted to accomplish in my life. I had
always feared that Ed would sabotage me the day before I went

into the studio to record my voice forevermore. But, now, as I look around my apartment, I just do not see him anywhere. Of course, this means that he could be outside in the car setting an elaborate trap to get me in the morning. But as long as I keep recovery first, I will have the ability to safely cross that bridge when I come to it.

Going to Any Lengths

"WHAT ARE YOU willing to do?" Emily, a friend in group therapy, asked me over and over again. I began my true separation from Ed when my answer became, "I am willing to go to any lengths."

What am I willing to do? I follow all of the instructions of the health care professionals that I hire to help me. I save money to pay for these appointments by collecting coupons for everything from movies to food. And I actually go to the grocery store to buy the food listed on the coupons. I bring my own meals on airplanes, because peanuts and a diet coke don't satisfy the five food groups anymore. In the beginning, I had to push aside all of the Diet Dr Pepper bottles in my refrigerator to make room for some real food. I once stopped walking in a marathon at the halfway point, because lunch was not served at any of the Gatorade stations along the course. I even turned down a job interview when I didn't have time for both lunch and the appointment. Regardless of the circumstance, I am willing to go to whatever extent necessary to take care of my recovery and myself.

When I became "willing to go to any lengths," Ed quickly formulated a plan to fight me. His big plan entailed his also becoming "willing to go to any lengths." (He's not known for his original ideas.) But no matter what he does, I am always willing to go further. For instance, Ed proclaims, "If you eat dinner this late, you are going to gain ten pounds overnight right on your stomach." He always specifies body parts. To Ed's surprise, I am actually willing to gain the ten pounds, and I eat dinner. (For the record, I have never gained weight overnight due to eating a late dinner.) "Willing to go to any lengths" means that I will risk whatever threats Ed pulls out of thin air. What are you willing to do?

Grieving the Good

I DROVE TO BRETT's house with one thing in mind. I was going to break up with him. I had finally had enough of his controlling, abusive nature. I was going to get my life back. And that is just what I did.

I was so happy to be free. Everything was great. At the same time, I have to admit that there were things about my ex that I missed. I used to like hearing him sing and play guitar late at night, and I loved the way that he could make me laugh. I missed having someone to do special things for. When we broke up, I definitely got rid of all of the negative aspects of our relationship, but I also had to give up the good things.

It was no different when I decided to divorce Ed. There were certain things about him that I really missed. It was hard to live without that ability to instantly numb myself by bingeing. During a binge, I had no stress, I was separated from reality, and everything in the world seemed OK. I also had to cope with giving up purging, whether that meant throwing up, starving, or overexercising. Purging was my seemingly magic solution to bingeing and not gaining weight. It was relief. Of course, I missed the starvation high and that false feeling of being in control. And what I really missed about Ed was how he made me feel special. He told me that I was stronger than other people.

He said, "Other people are so weak, Jenni. They actually believe the big myth about food. They really think that they need to eat. They only wish that they could have your control."

When I first tried to leave Ed, I mistakenly thought that I could just get rid of the negative things about him. I was thrilled to let go of the insanity that he brought to my life. I was more than happy to leave behind the inability to concentrate and the depletion of my energy. And I could not wait for the day that I didn't have to constantly obsess about food and my body. I definitely wanted to get rid of all of the bad things, but I was not ready to let go of the good things. So I made compromises with Ed.

> **JENNI:** I am going to eat today, because that is what I need to do for my recovery. I need to eat so that I will have energy to sing and write.
>
> **ED:** OK fine. You can eat but not enough to make you gain even an ounce. If you gain weight, you will be a loser—nothing special.
>
> **JENNI:** OK. It's a deal.

My compromises did not work. For instance, in order to have the energy that I needed to follow my dreams and really live my life, I had to follow my food plan, which meant I had to gain weight.

No matter how hard I tried to just let go of Ed's negative qualities, I couldn't do it. I would inevitably find myself back in his arms again. So I finally decided to wholeheartedly commit to recovery, and I had to grieve the characteristics of Ed that I really liked. It was a long, difficult process.

Today I no longer miss the qualities about Ed that I had once desired. I have developed other things in my life that take the place of Ed. I don't need Ed to make me feel special anymore. I know that I am unique in a lot of ways—in my music, my writing, and in just being me. I don't need Ed for stress relief. Instead, I have techniques to deal with stress like dancing, yoga, and just breathing. I do not need any part of Ed anymore.

When I dumped my ex-boyfriend, he told me that I would regret it someday. Ed said the same thing. I am still waiting for that day. Until then, I will just keep living my life one day at a time and enjoying it each step of the way.

The Not-So-Fun Part

I AM STARING AT my healthy breakfast, which adequately satisfies my food plan. The last thing in the world that I want to do is eat. And the most important thing for me to do right now is eat. This is the not-so-fun part of recovery. To be brutally honest, this is the part that I hate. Following my food plan when Ed is screaming in my ear is both challenging and painful.

Other aspects of recovery have always been relatively fun to me. For instance, in individual sessions, it is not uncommon for me to play with baseball bats, sirens, or a puppet named the Should Monster. Sometimes I even learn magic tricks. And group therapy is always filled with laughter. We wear masks, do role-plays, and even tear pillows to shreds. It's fun talking to the girls and getting to know everyone. Sure, I have experienced intense moments in therapy where I've broken down into tears or released stored-up anger. But these moments made me feel better in the end and more at peace with myself. If recovery involved only therapy, I would be one happy camper and a healthy one at that.

But in the realm of eating disorder recovery, someone is always going to mention food. Eventually, all of the fun and games will end, and you will find yourself staring down a plate of food. You will know that you need to eat the food, but Ed will provide you with other options. His ideas will range from refusing to take even one bite to eating everything on the plate and much more. He may even have suggestions for an after-mealtime activity. And Ms. Perfectionist, who keeps a close eye on your size and shape, will scrutinize each piece of food that you put into your mouth. Eating the food will not be filled with pizzazz or magic. It will not be exciting. This is the not-so-fun part. It is also an essential part of recovery.

Getting on a good cycle with food is extremely difficult. If you are anything like me, you should expect lots of ups, downs, twists, and turns. But once you get on a regular eating plan, you will ultimately feel so tremendously free and full of energy.

So the next time you find yourself one-on-one with a well-balanced meal, don't try to liven it up a bit by making smiley faces out of your peas and carrots. Just eat the food and accept that, at first, it will not be a very gratifying experience. Eventually, it will be the aspect of recovery that rebuilds your life and gives you the ability to really live out your dreams. Ironically, it is the not-so-fun part of recovery that actually enables life to be so much fun in the end.

How Can You?

How can you think about going to the grocery store when air
planes just collided into the World Trade Center? How can
you worry about buying food for lunch when terrorists are attacking America? How can you be concerned about your food plan
when thousands of lives just vanished? These were Ed's questions
on September 11, 2001.

Ed often attempts to use a tragic situation to his benefit. He
tries to make me feel guilty for being in recovery by asking, "How
can you be so selfish at a time like this?" At different times in my
life, Ed has asked me these questions:

"How can you focus energy on recovery when twelve young
college students were just killed in a terrible accident?"

"How can you worry about the amount of protein in your dinner when your friend is battling an unknown illness?"

"How can you spend time in therapy when there is a sniper on
the loose killing innocent people?"

"How can you worry about breakfast when a bomb just exploded
in Oklahoma City?"

Ed does not hesitate to use other people's pain and suffering to
distract me from recovery. He says, "All you do is spend time on
yourself, always digging deeper, always trying to love yourself.
What about other people? What about the world? Recovery has
turned you into a very closed-minded and self-centered person,
Jenni." That is what Ed tells me.

In therapy, I learned that the best way I can be fully available
to others is to take excellent care of myself. When I am practicing
good recovery, I have a clear mind and can actually concentrate. I
am able to listen and empathize. I can provide true comfort to a

friend in need. I have more energy to put toward helping other people. I can do things like drive to visit a friend, drop a sympathy card in the mail, or even donate blood at the Red Cross. Recovery enables me to put my best foot forward.

When I am hanging out with Ed, I cannot truly be there for other people. I can focus on only one thing—food. I am thinking about how I can get more food, how I can get rid of food, or how I can avoid food. A friend may be crying in my arms, and all I can think about is the large bag of cookies that I am going to binge on later. Because my mind is so preoccupied with Ed, I am unable to truly listen and offer real support. The best I can do is pretend.

When tragedy strikes in the world, now I expect Ed to start hassling me. If there is a fire across town, Ed will say, "How can you worry about making your doctor's appointment when someone's home is in flames?" Or in response to world hunger, he might say, "How can you eat dinner when people are starving?" He will tell me over and over again that recovery is selfish.

In reality, Ed—not recovery—epitomizes selfishness. He is the one who will do anything, including lying, cheating, and stealing, to satisfy his own needs. He is the one who constantly disregards other people's feelings in order to meet his own goals. At the expense of everyone else, Ed makes sure that his desires are top priority every time.

So when Ed tells me that I am being selfish, I just tell him to take a good long look in the mirror. If he wants to see true selfishness, that's where he will find it.

Won't vs. Can't

THE WALLS ARE bouncing in and out. I am anxious about nothing in particular. I am anxious about everything. I am afraid. I do not remember how to breathe. I feel like immediate action needs to be taken. Time is running out. I want to numb myself. I want to get out of these shaking walls. And I know just how to get out—binge. But that would be turning to Ed for help. I won't do it. I can do it, but I won't.

In therapy, I learned the important distinction between "can't" and "won't." "Can't" suggests both that I do not have a choice and that I am not in charge of my life. "Won't" acknowledges that I have a choice and that I am in charge. When I say, "I won't binge," I am taking full responsibility for my actions. I am actively participating in my life and not just letting things happen to me. Sure, I could definitely call Ed, and he would tell me the perfect food to binge on. But, now, I won't do it. I choose to say no.

Ed hated it when I made the switch from "can't" to "won't." He preferred the times when I was not in charge of my life. Then, it was easier for him to sneak in and take over. When Ed would tell me, "Just skip this one meal. It's no big deal," I would reply, "No, I can't do it." Immediately, the "can't" indicated to Ed that he had some pull in whether or not I starved myself. And he knew that I was not running the show. Ed would say, "Sure you can. All you have to do is tell everyone that you already ate lunch." And most of the time I would take his advice. Now, I tell Ed, "No. I won't do it." The simple exchange of "won't" for "can't" indicates that I am in charge. I am making the decision to follow my food plan—no questions asked.

So, as I sit here today, the walls are moving in and out around me. Ed still wants me to binge:

ED: Jenni, those walls will stop shaking if you just open that refrigerator door.
JENNI: I won't do it.
ED: Sure, you can.
JENNI: I know I can.
ED: Then, what's the problem?
JENNI: I won't.
ED: You can.
JENNI: I won't.

I played my trump card. Ed does not have a chance.

Realistic

MAKE NO MISTAKE—given the opportunity, Ed will kill you. Out of all of the reasons to divorce Ed, this is the most important one. Eating disorders have the highest mortality rate of any psychological illness. The records often do not show that Ed's victims died of anorexia or bulimia. Instead, it is reported that they died of cardiac arrest, kidney failure, or other medical complications. As you already know, it is not about food; it is about your entire being—mentally and physically. Sure, Ed starts off slow— just limiting what you eat here and there. But the raindrops quickly become a hurricane.

If you are like me, you are thinking, "I don't binge and purge that often," "It won't happen to me," or "I've lived like this for years." When I was surfing on the Internet one day, I learned that these are the same thoughts running through the minds of lots of girls who suffer with eating disorders. These were the thoughts of fifteen-year-old Kristen when she energetically headed off to camp one weekend in May. On Monday, Kristen was back at home, and her parents found her lifeless on her bed. Ed had gone too far; the paramedics never picked up a heartbeat.

You may also be thinking, "It won't happen to me," "I'm fat," or "I'm a normal weight." This is just how Ed manipulates you into thinking that he is not that big of a deal. He'll say, "How could you even think that you could die? You are definitely not rail-thin. You have meat on your bones." The fact is that even the doctors had said that Kristen was a normal, healthy weight, but she died anyway.

Ed does not discriminate by weight, age, gender, or any other factor. The same day that I read about Kristen on the Internet, I also learned about Melissa, Stephanie, Matt, Deborah, Chantel, and Andrea—all who lost their lives to eating disorders. Their families and friends had created websites in their memory. Even though Ed has taken many lives, he has not won. We must learn from Kristen, Melissa, and all of Ed's other victims. We must learn that no matter what Ed says about his intentions, he will destroy us if we let him. Put this knowledge to work motivating your divorce proceedings. A divorce from Ed is more than just the end of an abusive relationship—it is a decision to live.

The Minority Rule

WHAT IF YOU don't care if Ed kills you? Even if the threat of death does not scare you, there is still a small part inside of you that wants to live. How do I know this? The fact that you are reading this book proves that something inside of you does not want to die. Something inside of you yearns for recovery. You may not hear this part at all, because the large part of you that does not care about living is screaming very loudly in your head. You will need to listen carefully for that small voice that wants to fight for your life.

This part won't scream, "Recovery is great! Yeah life!" No, it will more likely say, "Maybe this whole recovery thing is possible. Just maybe my life is worth it."

Your motivation in recovery does not need to be huge in the beginning. Right now, you might just find enough motivation each day to bring you to the next day. Your motivation might be a fun evening that you have planned in the future. It might be a commitment to a friend or even an upcoming movie.

Many girls in my therapy group find their motivation in the fact that other people care about them. They are willing to continue on with recovery and do the next right thing in order to prevent their family and friends from hurting. Maybe you can find your motivation to live in other people, too.

Or maybe you are like other girls in my therapy group who believe that no one cares about them. In one group session, Kim said with confidence, "I feel so alone. No one in the world cares whether I am alive or dead. I might as well be dead."

Immediately other girls argued with Kim. Someone said, "Kim, that's not true. People do care about you."

Hilary added, "We all care so much about you."

Kim just shrugged her shoulders and said, "I just don't believe it. I feel really isolated from everyone."

Thom apparently knew that there was no point in trying to convince Kim of something that she did not believe, so he took the conversation in a different direction. "Kim," he said, "You said that you feel alone. What does that feel like?"

Kim slowly answered, "It feels cold and scary." Tears started rolling down her face as she continued, "Being so alone makes me so depressed. I feel worthless."

Thom gave Kim time to express her emotions, and he encouraged the rest of us to listen and not try to talk Kim out of her feelings. A little later he asked Kim, "How are you feeling now? Are you feeling alone?"

"Actually," Kim said, "I feel a little better, more connected to the group. It's nice to talk about this stuff with people who understand."

Often when someone expresses previously held-back emotions in group, that individual feels closer to everyone in the room. This feeling of connectedness helps people become aware that group is a family that truly cares about its members.

Kim left group that night with what I have heard Thom call "reasonable doubt." Maybe, just maybe, she wasn't a lost cause. Maybe the women in the group did really care about her.

If you feel the same way that Kim did at the beginning of group, it might help you to talk to someone you trust and express your feelings. You might want to talk about feelings of loneliness or depression. Sharing your emotions with another individual will enable you to feel a little closer to that person. You might even walk away from the conversation believing that it is possible that someone does care about you. You might develop reasonable doubt.

Of course, in the long run, the goal is not to live your life for someone else. But if another person caring about you gives you motivation to stay on the planet and keep trying for now, that's fine. Whatever works. What motivates you now does not have to be what motivates you down the line. Someday you will be motivated to live for yourself and not for someone else.

To stay in recovery, you must be responsible for finding your own motivation. Remember, motivation may not be easy to come by at first. It will probably be a very small, timid part inside of you. When you find it, let that part be in charge. Let the minority rule and lead you to a life that you never dreamed was possible.

Duct Tape

SOME BOOKS SUGGEST putting locks on the refrigerator door and kitchen cabinets in order to prevent bingeing. I never tried this, because I lived alone and could trust neither Ed nor myself with the key. Instead, I put long strips of duct tape across the entrance to my kitchen; that's right, I taped myself out. And I actually believed that this brilliant contraption would stop me the next time I wanted to binge and purge.

Then, it came—that "walls are closing in" feeling. I was anxious about nothing in particular and about everything. I panicked. I forgot how to breathe. Immediate, yet temporary, relief screamed for me from the kitchen. It was Ed. Somehow he had gotten past the duct tape blockade. "Jen, come on in," and he motioned for me to join him beyond the gray tape.

It took me all of two seconds to tear down the barrier that I had put so much confidence in earlier that evening (and not that much earlier). I'm pretty sure that spending the extra buck for the heavy-duty tape would not have helped.

Whenever I had that horrible feeling that precedes a binge, I wanted instant relief. I tried everything. I soaked binge food in water. Then, I went to the store to buy more food to binge on. Sometimes, I tried drinking diet soda instead of bingeing. I walked back and forth from the refrigerator and grabbed can after can of diet soda. Inevitably, on one trip to the refrigerator, my hand would grab a block of cheese, raw biscuit dough, and peanut butter instead.

Why couldn't I find one action that would make the need to binge automatically disappear? Because there is no magic action to make that horrible prebinge feeling go away. The cool thing is that we are designed so that the feeling will pass through us on its own—in time. All we have to do is sit there and feel what is going on inside of us. We must experience the feelings. To help us deal with the feelings, we can call someone on our support team. We can also express the feelings by focusing on our breath or even hitting a pillow. The important thing to remember is that no matter how terrible, feelings do pass. It takes patience and trust—not food, and definitely not duct tape.

Bones

JULIE CAME INTO group one night and told everyone about her recent diagnosis at the doctor's office. "I just got my bone density scan results back, and I have osteoporosis," she said.

Osteoporosis is a disease characterized by the loss of bone tissue. I thought that it was a disease that affected only older people, but I was wrong. Julie is in her twenties. I was surprised to learn that night in our discussion that young people with eating disorders are at a considerably increased risk for developing the disease.

When Julie told us about her diagnosis, I learned that several other girls in the group also have been diagnosed with osteoporosis. Still others in the group have osteopenia, which is the stage before true osteoporosis. As we talked that night, I remembered that Dr. Tucker had recommended that I get a bone density scan more than a year before. I didn't think I could possibly have anything wrong with my bones and I didn't want to deal with filing an insurance claim, so I never scheduled the test. After sitting through that group session, however, I called Dr. Tucker the next day and set up an appointment for the test.

Weeks later I came home to a message on my answering machine from Dr. Tucker. He told me that I have osteopenia. Only months earlier, my mom had had a bone density scan. She is in her fifties and has optimal bone density. Meanwhile, I am in my twenties and have thinning bones. I told my mom that day, "I don't want to live my life being permanently hunched over."

Then I started to read as much information as I could on osteoporosis, and I realized that progressively stooping for the rest of my life is only one of my worries. The skeletal crumbling of osteoporosis interferes with one's ability to eat and get around independently. When osteoporosis interacts with other health problems, it often leads to death. Half of the people who break a hip will never walk again unaided, and of those older than fifty, a quarter will die within a year.

After realizing what poor condition my bones were in and what might lie ahead for me, I immediately got mad at myself. "Why didn't you take care of yourself? Strong bones run in your family, but you ruined yours. Why did you starve and deprive yourself for all of those years?" I quickly realized that I needed to be asking Ed those questions and not myself. Ed is the one who convinced me to damage my body. Ed is the one who thought being thin was more important than anything else—obviously more important than my bones.

I often think that I wish someone had told me about my risk for osteoporosis when I was active in my eating disorder. I honestly did not know that I was hurting my body. I thought that I was young and my body was resilient. I thought that I could do anything. I just did not know. That is why I am telling you now. I want you to have the choice that I did not have. You can commit to recovery and protect your body or you can continue with Ed and risk developing osteopenia, osteoporosis, or other health problems.

If I had had the knowledge that you now have, who knows what I would have done with it? Ed would have probably told me, "Jenni, it won't happen to you. You aren't that bad off. Your bones are fine." And I might have continued on my journey with Ed just as I did. But just maybe I would have really thought about what I was doing to my body. Maybe I would have worried enough about my health and at least looked into recovery sooner than I did. I will never know what I would have done.

But that is not important. What really matters now is you. What are you going to do with the information that you now have? Don't listen to Ed when he says that it won't happen to you. Don't listen to him when he says, "You are not emaciated enough to have problems with your bones."

Women of all shapes and sizes in my support group developed osteopenia and osteoporosis. Even if you are just flirting with Ed, you are at an increased risk for these diseases. Don't believe Ed when he tells you that you are not. He is lying. It happened to me, and it has happened to lots of women and men all over the world. It can happen to you, too. Don't let it.

Trapped

"GATORADE OR THE hospital," Susan said.

I had a choice. I could drink a Gatorade or go to the hospital to be given fluids intravenously. I definitely did not want to go to the hospital. But Ed was not allowing me to eat or drink anything, so the Gatorade was also out of the question.

"Gatorade or the hospital," Susan repeated again. "What's it going to be?" she asked.

I did not want to answer her question. All I really wanted to do was to get out of Susan's office as soon as possible. I wanted to get in my car, drive away, and avoid her question altogether. But I could not leave, because I did not have my car at her office. My vocal coach, Judy, had driven me to the appointment, and she was not about to let me walk away. I was trapped.

As Susan continued to talk to me—reviewing my two choices—I kept searching for a way out. I stared at Susan's window contemplating whether or not I could escape that way. I figured that I could break through the window and walk home. You are probably wondering why I did not just walk out of the door instead of planning to break through the window. After all, Judy and Susan would not have physically forced me to stay. It is clear to me now that I could have certainly just stood up and walked out the door. But in that moment, Ed was in the room and in control. And the window is the way he wanted me to go. It would be much more exciting and dramatic to break through the glass, scale my way down the wall from her second floor office, and walk all the way home—exhausted. So that is what I wanted to do.

Ed was running the show, and I was not thinking rationally. Ed made it clear that Judy and Susan were out to get me. He said that they just wanted to make me fat and ruin my life. "I hate you," I yelled at them. They were surprised by my harsh statement but were unwavering in their position. They were not going to let me off of the hook. At the time, the concept of tough love was lost on me. Now I understand what it meant for them to risk my hating them.

As Susan continued to ask me what I wanted to do—Gatorade or the hospital—Ed and I were having an intense conversation:

> ED: Whatever you do, you cannot let them force you to put fluids into your body. If you do that, you will blow up like a blimp. Today is a non-eating day, and you are not allowed to eat anything. That means no liquid either. Nothing.
>
> JENNI: Ed, I do not really have a choice. I have to answer Susan's question. What should it be—the Gatorade or the hospital?
>
> ED: You do not have to answer the question. Just keep avoiding it. Get up and leave.
>
> JENNI: But I am paying Susan to help me. Why should I even bother coming to her office if I am not going to listen to what she has to say?
>
> ED: Susan just wants to make you fat. That is what she is in the business of doing—making people fat. Get out of here.
>
> JENNI: Ed, you got me in this situation in the first place. I think I need to quit listening to you and actually trust someone else.

So I finally answered Susan's question. It was not easy, but I decided that I would drink the Gatorade. That was a very tough decision to make.

In recovery, you will face many difficult questions. Some of the questions will be in the form of options given to you by your health care professionals. Some of them will be questions that you ask yourself. Others will come from friends, family members, and even Ed.

Do not worry about getting all of the answers right. Sometimes there will not be a right or wrong answer. Sometimes it is just important that you face the issue at hand (instead of sneaking out of the window). For instance, it did not really matter whether I chose Gatorade or the hospital. Either way I was going to be giving myself the fluids that my body needed. The important thing was that I answer the question and face the fact that I needed to take care of my body.

As long as you are facing the issues in your recovery head-on, you will be moving forward. And you won't have to worry about breaking any windows.

Thom's Turn

1. The Good and Bad About Ed

Once Jenni became really serious about getting better, she had to face the fact that there were some things about Ed that she was going to miss. The truth is that she could not get rid of just the bad things about Ed. She had to *give up* the good things in order to *get rid of* the bad. Ed made Jenni feel special and offered her comfort. Jenni had to move forward with her recovery without knowing whether she would ever feel special again. It was a real loss and had to be grieved.

Consider the good and bad parts of your eating disorder. Divide a sheet of paper down the middle. On one side, make a list of all of the things that you want to keep about Ed, the things you know you will miss once you are in recovery. Maybe your eating disorder offers you temporary relief in stressful situations. Maybe it helps you feel in control.

On the other side of the sheet of paper, list all of the things about Ed that you will be happy to get rid of. Think about everything your eating disorder has taken from you—including everything it has kept you from having in the first place. For instance, has your eating disorder kept you from having meaningful relationships? Has it prevented you from following your dreams? This is a very important list to make—sometimes called a "loss list." Be specific and thorough.

Be willing to make several trips to these lists as your awareness increases and especially as you become better and better at confronting your eating disorder.

2. Disobeying Your Eating Disorder

After you have learned how to separate from your eating disorder, distinguishing your thoughts, feelings, and beliefs from those of the eating disorder, it is time to take a stand. It is time to listen to what the eating disorder is telling you to do, and then refuse to do it!

Let's practice.

- Write some of the suggestions, recommendations, or commands your eating disorder has given you over the past couple of days.
- Write a couple of good examples of how you have been responding to what your eating disorder has been telling you to do. (Include mental, verbal, emotional, and action responses.)
- Write a strong statement that is characteristic of your eating disorder, and then write an even stronger statement from you, refusing to obey! (You don't have to mean it, or even feel it—this is just practice.)

3. The Terrifying Experiment

You are very familiar with what Ed tells you to do throughout the day. Like Jenni, you may also hear other voices daily, including the voice of Ms. Perfectionist or some other expert inner critic. None of this, of course, is news to you.

It is time now—believe it or not—to add another voice to the mix. And very often, this new voice proves more difficult, and even more painful, than Ed or the other messages in your head. This new voice is a challenge because it is something you are not used to. What is unfamiliar can seem quite treacherous. The new voice that you are about to add to the mix is a compassionate voice, a kind voice, a supportive voice. Before you go any further, make a few notes about your initial reaction to the idea of such a voice. It is not unusual to experience resistance, fear, and even anger at the suggestion of self-compassion.

Now, for the next week, try this:

Once a day write down five compassionate statements to yourself. For instance, give yourself credit for something you accomplished or learned that day, or acknowledge your positive intentions or heartfelt efforts even when things do not turn out well. Whatever you write, make it positive and supportive. And on one day when you are feeling particularly brave, try writing something to yourself that is loving. During one day in Jenni's recovery, she wrote the following compassionate statements to herself:

1. Jenni, I was so proud of you today when you were honest with your friend about not wanting to go to the concert.
2. You really were brave today when you expressed your anger during group.
3. You took care of yourself today. Even though Ed was screaming in your ear, you had the strength to stay in recovery.
4. I admire how you took time out of your busy workday to eat a relaxing lunch with a friend outside.
5. Jenni, you gave great support to Darcy today. Way to go!

It is OK to repeat statements from one day to the next (e.g., I really respect how you are sticking to this exercise every day), but try to come up with some new material each day. And do not worry about whether you really mean the kind, compassionate statements to yourself. For now, just write them down—think of it as a strange and terrifying experiment.

Here are a couple more ideas: 1) Consider writing the exercises in this section and others as a note in your smartphone. The "Emergency 911 Card" exercise in part 5 (page 138) would work well as a note, too. Think of this as recovery in your pocket—with you wherever you go. 2) Exercise 1 in this section can be completed online using websites like proconlists.com. On the Internet, you can actually weigh the pros and cons of Ed based on factors like emotions and rationality. (Since Ed is so irrational, he really hates this system; he often loses out.)

7

BELIEVE IT

What It's All About

Life without Ed is truly amazing. I no longer spend all of my time obsessing about food and my body. I can now focus on what really matters to me in life. Genuine, lasting recovery from an eating disorder is about true independence. Keep moving forward, and you will find that freedom. Part 7 is what it is all about.

I'm Not Perfect

I WAKE UP EVERY morning happy to be alive. I am happy to be free and not ruled by Ed. I am thrilled that I no longer have to squeeze myself into a tiny glass box every day—smiling as the air in the box is used up. I am very happy, but I am not perfect. Ed still shows his face every once in a while. The difference between now and years ago is that when Ed shows up today, I do not give him my power.

Ed still tells me on occasion, "Your jeans feel loose. Just think how good it would feel if you lost weight and those jeans hung even lower on your waist." Then he helpfully adds, "I can help you get there." I listen to what Ed has to say. Then, I tell him, "no," and I go on with what I am doing. And because I'm not perfect, sometimes I hesitate before I say no.

Today, I am not Ed-free. But Ed is no longer a parasite on my flesh sucking out my energy and passion. Ed is just that guy who throws out predictable random comments that have nothing to do with who I am. They have nothing to do with Jenni.

I like to think of Ed's appearance in my life today as a test of the emergency broadcast system on television and radio. You know—that loud, sustained beep that comes on once in a while in the middle of normal programming? It is annoying, but you know that it will be short-lived. And most important, it is not a real emergency, just a reminder that you need to know what to do in the case of an actual emergency.

What Kept Me Going?

WHEN I WAS crumpled in a ball by the toilet, what picked me up off the floor? What lifted me out of bed when I felt as if I was being run over by an eighteen-wheeler? What opened the window shades and let the sunlight into my gloomy apartment? What kept me going? Brief moments of freedom from my eating disorder kept me moving along the recovery path. These glimpses into what my life could be like without Ed were like precious jewels to me. I held onto these instances and used them as fuel for when I really wanted to give up.

What moments of freedom am I talking about? Going out to lunch with a friend and actually having a good time; daydreaming for five minutes without thoughts of food or weight passing through my mind; tasting a truffle for the first time at a chocolate shop and not feeling guilty; passing by Wendy's at 2:00 A.M. (enough said); the energy to do one sit-up; the power to reach a high note in a song; noticing the colors of the beautiful flowers in my neighbor's garden; looking at myself in the mirror and liking what I see.

Even walking through the frozen-food aisle of the grocery store without feeling like an icicle is a time to remember. When I was hand in hand with Ed, the world was always so cold—physically and emotionally.

I wrote in my journal about how good I felt when I was not living under Ed's control. Then, when I really felt like giving up, I read these pages and realized that what I was striving for in recovery was a real possibility. I thought about these experiences and used them as encouragement to keep moving forward. Even one minute of freedom was proof that I was getting better. At first, these times were few and far between. Now, these moments are connected; they are my life.

No

AFTER A LONG day at work, all I wanted to do was spend some quiet time alone at home writing. As soon as I sat down on the couch and picked up my pen, the phone rang.

"Hello," I said.

"Hey, Jenni. It's Danny. There's a great party going on tonight. Get ready, and I'll pick you up in thirty minutes."

The last thing in the world that I wanted to do was go to a party, so, of course, I answered, "Sounds great. I'll be waiting for you."

I just could not say no. I did not want to hurt Danny's feelings. If I had said no, he might have hated me forever. And Ms. Perfectionist works diligently to assure that no one ever hates me. So I put my pen and paper down and got ready for a party that I really did not want to go to.

That scene happened years ago in my pre-no phase, the large part of my life during which I could not say no. Saying no meant feeling guilty, so I always said yes.

One of the coolest things I have learned in recovery is the ability to use that simple word, *no*. Being in recovery gave me the confidence to use this small but powerful word. I learned that saying no to someone was not likely to negatively affect that relationship forever. And I realized that if it did, then something was wrong with that relationship in the first place. Today saying no is an important tool in my life. When I use it, I know that I am taking care of myself.

Ironically, if you want to add "no" to your vocabulary, first you must say yes. You must say yes to recovery. Say yes, and before you know it, you'll be saying no.

Double Take at the Fridge

P APER OR PLASTIC? This used to be the biggest decision that I made at the grocery store. I did not have to decide what to buy, because Ed already had that figured out for me. My grocery list was always the same—apples, bagels, and Diet Dr Pepper. Today, the grocery store is quite a different story. I can no longer stand in the express lane with my three little items. Not anymore.

These days, I often do a double take at my refrigerator. I am so amazed when I open it up and see things like eggs, milk, sandwich meat, and cheese that I often have to look twice just to be certain. Sometimes I even check all around me to make sure that I am standing in the right house and looking in the right refrigerator. In the past, I would have had no use for "superfluous" items like milk and cheese. I did not need these things to survive, and that is all that I was interested in—surviving. Taste did not matter. Nutrition did not matter. Nothing else mattered. I did not wake up and wonder, "What do I feel like eating for breakfast today?" Because it did not matter what I felt like. I had no choices. If I was actually eating breakfast that day, it was going to be a bagel. End of discussion. No questions asked.

Today, I actually have options. Sometimes, I still might eat a bagel as a part of my breakfast, but I do not have to—I choose to. I actually enjoy trying new things—like various types of cereal, new flavors of yogurt, different kinds of fruits, and even things like pancakes. And I feel so much healthier now that I am supplying my body with a variety of nutrients. I have more energy, can think a hundred times more clearly, and am much happier.

Where is Ed in all of this? Ed still goes to the grocery store with me sometimes. He looks at me in disbelief when I reach for things like butter or a loaf of bread. And of course, he tells me how fat I am going to get if I eat those things. "Butter," he says, "What in the world do you need butter for?" He has no idea that butter actually makes some things taste really good.

Eventually, Ed always says, "Well, if you are going to buy all of this food anyway, you might as well go all out and plan a huge binge." He gets excited and tries to throw extra items into the cart. Today I have the strength to just ignore him.

I also am able to ignore Ed when he tries to get me confused in the store over the various labels on food these days: fat free, 99 percent fat free, 98 percent fat free, 98.5 percent fat free, reduced fat, extra reduced fat, low-fat, no fat, reduced calorie, extra reduced calorie, low-calorie, no calorie, o calorie. He will do his best to get me all worked up about the difference between "no calorie" and "o calorie" or "fat free" and "no fat," but I do not obsess about those words anymore. I leave all of the worrying to Ed. He can spend a surprisingly long period of time in the store just standing in one place staring at all of the different labels and trying to make sense of them. While he is busy studying the labels, I am often able to finish shopping all by myself—without Ed's constant criticism.

I quickly decide paper or plastic and leave Ed counting calories.

Dividing the Marital Property

W HEN IT WAS time to divide the marital property, I decided to take charge. I returned to Ed every gift that he had ever given to me. For instance, it was not hard to part with that book given for my eighteenth birthday titled, *101 Ways to Treat Yourself Worse than Your Worst Enemy*. I also let him have the audio book that he thought was such a great gift one Christmas: *If You Didn't Feel Guilty, You Do Now*. Neither of us got that metal contraption, Ed's favorite instrument of torture—the scale—because I destroyed it with my trusty hammer and put it out for garbage pickup early one morning.

As far as I am concerned, Ed is not taking anything away from our marriage that I need. I let him have all of the self-hatred. He can have his treasured shame. And he can certainly keep his "support system" of extreme codependents, manipulative ex-boyfriends, and addicts who don't want anything to do with recovery. After all, these were the people whom Ed had encouraged me to call when I was in desperate need of support. He always wanted me to look for approval where I was least likely to get it. Ed can have them; I don't need them. I never needed them.

So what am I taking away from our marriage? I have all of the self-compassion. I am taking the honesty and integrity. (I no longer need to lie to cover up for Ed.) I got the support system of friends in recovery and health care professionals. I have the willingness and energy to treat myself well. I am taking the happiness, love, and freedom. Most of all, I am walking away with my life and my future.

Ed and I still have not decided who is going to get the can opener. I need it to open canned vegetables and tuna fish. But Ed says that he just could not survive without the ability to open his favorite item—a can of worms.

The Chosen One

D O YOU EVER feel as if you are the only person in the world who cannot recover from your eating disorder? I used to think that it was possible for everyone else to get better, but not me. I thought that I was that one special case—the one person who was truly incapable of leaving Ed. We had been together for so long. He had always controlled my thoughts and actions. I thought that nothing would ever change.

"I just don't think I will ever be able to let go of Ed. I think I am the only one who won't succeed at recovery," I said to the girls in group one night.

Melissa responded, "I know exactly what you mean. I feel as if all of you guys will get rid of Ed and move on with your lives, and I will still be here in this room all by myself."

Mary jumped in the conversation: "I don't think so. I will be the one here all alone."

Everyone in the room started saying the same things. We each thought that we were the one case that was incapable of recovery. It's funny. We all think we are unique in this negative way—never being able to recover. But we do not label ourselves as being so special in some other positive way. For instance, I don't claim to be the best singer in the world. I am not the smartest person on the planet. But when it comes to my eating disorder, I am the best. My Ed is the most powerful. I am the one individual who will fail at recovery. But after years of struggling, I have divorced Ed. So have Melissa, Mary, and many others in our group. And still others are well on their way.

You are no different from me or anyone else. Don't get me wrong. You are special. You are unique in your personality and spirit and in just being you. But in your eating disorder, you are like the rest of us. You are not the chosen one destined to live with Ed forever. After all, I used to be that person. So did Melissa, Mary, and millions of others. And look where we are now. Come and join us.

Don't Give Up

I AM ALONE IN my apartment curled up on the couch with a blanket. It is quiet. Three lamps provide enough lighting for me to write, and a large candle with four wicks sits on the table in front of me. It is the evening of Thanksgiving. There are leftovers in the refrigerator, and I am not afraid. I am calm. I am peaceful. Even the white chocolate raspberry cheesecake is not calling my name. Unlike times in the past, I have not doused all of the food in water and thrown it into the trash can in order to avoid a binge. In fact, I was not even thinking about the food until I pleasantly realized that I was not thinking about the food. This is why it is worth it to never give up—the ability to enjoy silence and not be tormented by what I have eaten today and by what remains in the refrigerator to be eaten.

Years ago, Thanksgiving Day was quite a different story. I was so proud that I had not eaten a bite the entire day. Of course, no one knew except me. I did not have any leftovers in my refrigerator, because I was too scared to keep anything in my refrigerator except Diet Dr Pepper. If I was alone in my apartment, I was so hungry that I did not have the brainpower to be still and concentrate on anything. If I was not hungry, it was because I had just finished bingeing on something that I had picked up at the grocery store or a nearby drive-through. Years ago, I thought the reality of what I am doing right now was impossible. I wanted to give up. I was hopeless. But, I did not quit. And things sometimes got worse before they got better. And then after they got better, they got worse again. Finally, each day became better than the last. I kept putting one foot in front of the other. I took some of these steps kicking and screaming. But the pain was worth it. It led me to where I am now—relaxing and taking the time to write on this Thanksgiving night. If you don't give up, you will find peace, too. Whenever you come really close to throwing in the towel, just throw something at Ed instead. He makes a great target.

For inspiration to keep going, subscribe to positive social media news feeds or join pro-recovery e-newsletters. See Resources at the end of the book for links to my social media sites, and join my newsletter at jennischaefer.com.

Serenity

WITHIN THE WALLS of my support group, I often heard the word *serenity*. I always wondered, "Does serenity really exist?" Because Ed used to sit on my lap during group therapy sessions, he would quickly answer my question: "Sure. You experience that thing all of the time. Remember your binge last night? Just think of how numb you felt. You didn't have a care in the world. And today, as soon as that starvation high kicks in, you'll be floating in the sky."

After years in recovery, I finally found true serenity right here on the ground—not up in the clouds with Ed. It is truly amazing, and I thank God for it daily. What is serenity? I will begin by describing what it is not.

It is not obsessing about dinner before even eating breakfast. It is not scrambling for food in order to fill a bottomless hunger. It is not sitting on my kitchen floor feeling guilty and depressed after what I have just done. It is not staring down a toilet with tears streaming down my face. It is not giving all of my food away to a friend and making a promise to myself to never eat again. It is not feeling guilty for taking care of myself. It is not people pleasing. It is not Ms. Perfectionist. It is not Ed.

So, what is serenity? It is actually eating on Thanksgiving Day. It is enjoying myself at a cookout. It is being alone in my apartment without being afraid. It is having the energy to walk around the block. It is letting go. It is letting people get close to me and my boundaries. It is honesty. It is being able to say no. It is the ability to focus. It is the passion to pursue my dreams. It is having so much more time for living. It is me. And it can be you, too.

Dreams

"I DID IT! I made my first solo flight," Lajuana said in group one night. She had always wanted to be a pilot, but for thirty years, Ed had stopped her. Through recovery, Lajuana had found her wings.

That same night, Beth was sitting in the corner of the room holding her first baby in her lap.

"I never thought I would be able to have a child," she said, "but now I am able to take excellent care of her and myself."

Later on, Nikki announced to everyone that she had finally made the decision to quit the family business that she had worked in her entire life.

She said, "I'm going back to school like I always wanted to do."

Recovery is not only a commitment to fight Ed; it is a decision to listen to your heart and follow your dreams. When Ed was front and center in my world, I lost sight of what I really wanted out of life. All that seemed to matter was food and weight. I was so lost that I almost followed a completely different path in life. Ed was screaming so loud in my head that I could not hear the part of myself that wanted to sing and write.

Don't ever let anyone tell you that dreams don't come true. Especially don't let Ed tell you that what you really want out of life is impossible. It may very well be impossible if Ed is running the show, but once he is knocked out of the driver's seat, you will see that anything can happen. I see that every week when I look around at the faces of the women who sit with me in group therapy. And I see that every day when I look in the mirror.

Life Without Ed

I REMEMBER THE first time I learned that orange juice has calories. I was only a little girl. I used to love to drink a glass of orange juice every evening. At that time, I did not know that liquid had calories, so I thought that I could drink as much orange juice as I wanted without gaining weight. When someone told me that orange juice did, in fact, have calories, I ended my nightly orange juice ritual immediately. That was life with Ed.

I remember shopping for my high school prom dress. What mattered most was not the color, length, or neckline. The most important element of the dress was the number on the tag inside of it. I just wanted to fit into the smallest size available on the rack. All I really cared about was the size that I wore and how thin I looked in the dress. That was life with Ed.

I remember falling asleep on my kitchen floor after eating so much that it hurt to stand up. I would wake up the next day to a complete mess in the kitchen. Food was everywhere. I always cleaned everything up as if nothing had ever happened, and I vowed never to eat again. That was just life with Ed.

So what is life without Ed? It is waking up in the morning and drinking a tall glass of orange juice without feeling guilty. It is shopping for clothes that I really like and that I feel good in. It is not obsessing about the size. And it is cooking in my kitchen—not sleeping in it.

But those things only scratch the surface of what life without Ed is like. It is so much more than orange juice and clothing. Life without Ed is being true to yourself. It is honoring your mind, spirit, and body. It is the ability to make goals and chase after your dreams. Life without Ed is waking up every morning and being so happy to be alive.

And life without Ed is worth it. It is worth all of the pain that goes along with recovery. It is worth feeling fat for a little while or for as long as it takes. Recovery is worth constantly driving to and from therapy, dietitian, and doctor appointments. It is worth the struggle, the relapses, and the feelings of hopelessness.

Life without Ed is definitely the road less traveled. It would be easy for you to close this book and continue with all of your eating disorder behaviors. It would be simple to let Ed control you for the rest of your life. It's not difficult to let Ed make all of your decisions and to use him to get out of dealing with your feelings. The hard thing to do is to get on the recovery path and make a commitment to never get off no matter what you may confront. The real challenge is to let other people support you on your journey. And I challenge you to have some fun along the way. Learn about yourself, try new things, and let people get close to you.

Earlier I said that not allowing myself to drink orange juice as a child was just life with Ed. But when I think about it, there is really no such thing as life with Ed. Because being enmeshed with Ed and thinking about food and weight all of the time is not really living. Harming your body over and over again without thinking about the consequences is not living. It is quite the opposite. It is dying.

I decided that I wanted to live. You opened up this book because something inside of you wants to live, too. Something inside of you wants to experience all of the vast possibilities in this world. If you divorce Ed, you will be able to do anything. You will be able to make your wildest dream come true. You can change careers, go to school, or even pack up all of your things and move. You can learn a foreign language, make new friends, or get to truly know your old ones.

Life without Ed is what I hope for you. I hope that you will experience the amazing world that I live in today. I hope that the colors will come back into your life, the birds will sing, and the wind will blow through your hair. And I hope you feel it. I hope you feel the freedom that awaits you. Believe in yourself, and you will find it. You will find a life without Ed.

AFTERWORD

Ten Years Later

Thanks to recovery, my eating disorder has been among the best gifts in my life—albeit one that arrived in the absolute ugliest package. Words cannot adequately describe the pain and frustration that come alongside an eating disorder, and, similarly, nothing can possibly depict the true miracle of recovery. Don't quit before this miracle happens for you. And that is exactly what this afterword is all about: never giving up and pushing through, *all the way*, to a complete recovery. Here you will also find sections for males, loved ones, health care professionals, as well as an actual divorce decree to sign. If you haven't already, consider signing your name to it. A full recovery takes a full commitment. You can do it.

Life After Ed

E D WASN'T TOO happy that I wrote this book exposing the truth about his lies and manipulative tactics. In fact, it seemed as though my ex was so mad that he came back for retaliation after I turned the manuscript in to my publisher. Although this final fling with Ed was short-lived, it was also one of the most powerful—catapulting me into a newfound freedom that I never believed possible. At the time, unaware that this transformation was taking place, I was just very frustrated.

Saying that I felt like the biggest loser in the world is a major understatement. In the months while my publisher was working hard to turn my manuscript about recovery into an actual book that would be available in stores, I was dancing with Ed. I found it depressing and quite annoying when friends and family, who had read an early copy of the manuscript, suggested that I reread my own book. They said, "Jenni, you wrote a lot about falling down in *Life Without Ed*. You know what to do."

I did know what to do, but I wasn't doing it. There were all kinds of reasons why. *It's hard. It hurts. I'm scared and tired (no, exhausted).* And let's not forget one of the most powerful: *Maybe I can figure out a way to keep just a tiny itsy bitsy piece of Ed and still be happy.* Wrong. Believing this was setting me up for a mediocre sort of recovery. One big problem with mediocre is that it doesn't have staying power but eventually leads back to the eating disorder each and every time. Not to mention, who wants to settle for mediocre when a complete recovery is possible? Yes, it is! I didn't know that when I originally wrote this book, but I am living it now.

For long-lasting independence from my eating disorder, Ed could no longer be an option for how I dealt with life. Of course, the truth is that during those early years of recovery, Ed was, in fact, an option—a big one. Imagine a metaphorical restaurant menu that lists, rather than food, ways to cope with life. The "Self-Compassion Special," "Meditation Medley," and "Signature Support" entrees are all delicious selections for self-soothing, but the "Ed Deluxe" (one of those dishes that never quite comes out the way you order it) is also a choice. To get fully better, I came to terms with the fact that Ed is a forbidden menu item that I refuse to order. Sure, I *could* order it, but I *won't*. This is an appropriate use of restricting. I began to apply the same determination to recovery that, in the past, I had applied to limiting my food intake, trying to stay a certain size, and other eating disordered behaviors. It is amazing what can happen when you use your determination and intelligence for positive endeavors. (Just now, Ed might have chimed in, "Well, *you're* not intelligent," but some research actually suggests that individuals with eating disorders are more intelligent than the average person.) Rather than restricting food, you can learn to wisely apply your talents to restricting the eating disorder out of existence.

Commit to giving recovery your all. That's what I had to do—no holding back. Based on this book so far, you may be thinking that I had already given recovery everything I had. That is absolutely true for that point in my life. But, as I became stronger over time, my ability to make strides in recovery became even greater. You might look at it this way: at the end of kindergarten, you surely were not in a place to begin second grade. But, at the end of first grade, you were probably more than ready. After I finished writing *Life Without Ed*, I had essentially graduated from first grade. It was time for me to move on to second. I was ready then, but not before.

Even still, I have to admit that I couldn't help but feel as though I had somehow slid backward as I reread my manuscript those many years ago (yes, I took the suggestion of my friends and family). The last part of this book talks about how amazing life is without Ed, and there I was with Ed. *How could I not have lost ground?*

I worked hard to change my perspective and to ask a new question. *How am I growing?* A lapse in behaviors does not mean you are back at square one. If you are familiar with yoga, you know that sometimes you fall when trying a new pose, which indicates that you are growing and challenging yourself. I had just written a book about my recovery, which was certainly a challenge. I was about to share my story with the world, the biggest commitment to my recovery that I had ever made out loud. Writing a book is an enormous leap in being accountable, which is a sign of strength, not weakness. Falling down is often about building awareness, and standing up quickly can turn that awareness into momentum.

There are all kinds of examples in life where things seemingly get worse before they get better. I recently picked up a virus in a jam-packed airplane, and my body temperature skyrocketed. I felt awful, but my doctor actually seemed quite excited about my high fever. "Your body is doing exactly what it needs to do. You are getting better and very quickly," she enthusiastically explained. Her cheery disposition about my fever did not make me feel any better physically, but it did help to know that I was on the path to health. In a similar way, consider how muscle tissue breaks itself down, which can be quite painful, on its way to getting bigger and stronger. And wildfires are necessary in order for a forest to thrive. Such is the nature of life. The next time you feel as though you are only getting worse, remember that you might just be gaining the information that you need to move on to the next level of recovery. You might be headed to second grade! (If it helps you to relate better, imagine the step from high school to college, or choose another analogy altogether.)

Don't get me wrong: my discussion of setbacks here is not simply an excuse to relapse. In recovery, we must do our absolute best to make choices that support our health. When I hit a hurdle, I couldn't just say, "Oh well, Ed pushed me," as I fell flat on my face. When we make the separation from Ed, decisions about recovery fall squarely on our own shoulders. Ed is not in control, so we can't blame him. Sure, he might make all kinds of suggestions (for a while, he might never shut up), but we have the power to say no and to choose life instead. Becoming accountable for my own recovery was actually one of the main reasons for using the Ed metaphor. By the way, it is just a metaphor. Over the years, people have asked me, "Do you really hear voices?" No, but I will say that Ed screaming in my head was way more powerful than any audible voice could have been. Whether you relate to the Ed idea or not, you probably know what I mean by that negative voice. Some people who have read this book have chosen simply to refer to their eating disorder as "eating disorder," and that, of course, makes total sense. Do what works for you.

Regardless of what you call your eating disorder and what specific behaviors you struggle with, you absolutely can get better. Try not to use a specific eating disorder diagnosis (or lack thereof) as a reason to stay by Ed's side. (One of his favorite lines is "You aren't sick enough to deserve help.") Both males and females struggle with eating disorders ranging from anorexia nervosa and bulimia nervosa to binge eating disorder, OSFED (other specified feeding and eating disorders, formerly known as eating disorder not otherwise specified or EDNOS), and others. Make no mistake: eating disorders—even ones named with a complex acronym—are serious, life-threatening illnesses that deserve help. This topic is discussed in detail in my latest book, *Almost Anorexic: Is My (or My Loved One's) Relationship with Food a Problem?* (jennischaefer.com/books/almost-anorexic), which I cowrote with Jennifer J. Thomas, a clinical psychologist at Harvard Medical School. I didn't mention all of the various eating disorders by name in *Life Without Ed* previously, because I didn't know as much as I do now. As Maya Angelou says, "When you know better you do better."

Along my journey, part of "doing better" meant continually choosing recovery and setting myself up to be much more accountable for that choice. As I explained, writing this book was a big step for me in being responsible for my own recovery. But there are plenty of ways to be accountable without writing a book, which surely isn't the right path for everyone. I encourage you to risk making more commitments related to recovery and life. E-mail your food plan to someone your trust each morning, as described in part 2. Or make a promise to a friend that you will do something fun every single day, and send a text message as confirmation that you did it. Commit to journaling, and tell someone about your plans. If you don't enjoy writing, record your thoughts by using the voice memo feature on your phone instead. Consider online support; sign up for a free mentor at mentorconnect-ed.org and join in positive discussions on my Facebook page at Facebook.com/ LifeWithoutEd. If your supply of hope runs low, borrow some from me or someone else. There is plenty of hope to go around, which is crucial in staying accountable.

If your experience is anything like mine, you will have to make the choice to get better over and over again—even several times a minute on some days. What I can tell you (and I hope this will be a relief): ultimately, as with riding a bicycle, you will be able to take off your training wheels and ride with ease—without even thinking about it. Recovery will just become a natural, integrated part of your life. As an example, I eventually stopped using the metaphor of Ed altogether. It was just a tool—my training wheels—that gave me strength and assurance, particularly in early recovery, when separating from the eating disorder was such a key. In the beginning, fighting against Ed gave me a sense of separation and confidence. But eventually it became important for me to stop fighting against Ed so much. Sometimes I even spoke with him in a way that respected all that he had done for me, such as *Ed, I realize that you have tried to help me manage my life for years. Thank you, but I don't need you anymore.* And ultimately I began fighting for myself. I needed to practice great compassion toward my little girl, that invisible child inside of me—and eventually toward me as an adult. Different recovery tools became invaluable in these pursuits.

Spirituality is one. Ironically, a wholehearted commitment to recovery also meant fully letting go. It is impossible to control your body shape and size and everything else around you while simultaneously practicing good recovery. Trust me on that one. I tried. For me, letting go, which looks so easy on paper, was a huge task. It meant having more faith and trust in the people who were trying to help me. It required turning my heart to all things spiritual. To me, spirituality means, among other things, the faith and trust that I just referred to as well as music, nature, and prayer. Instead of writing letters to Ed, which was incredibly helpful early on, I wrote letters to God. I got in touch with my intuition, which I believe is my connection to God. What does spirituality mean to you? I didn't write about this topic in *Life Without Ed* up until now, because I didn't know how important it would become in order for me to reach a full recovery.

Speaking of letting go in a real physical way, I recently took a trapeze class in Austin, Texas, where I now live (yes, yet another music city). At the top of the ladder, the instructor, who was holding my belt firmly so I wouldn't fall, told me to lean completely forward—as in all the way—and grab the horizontal bar that was hanging high above the ground in front of me. She said to let go and stop thinking, which, naturally, got me thinking. But then, I remembered the idea of letting go. Many of the concepts that you learn in recovery will help you in life after Ed. And not just in trapeze class. When she yelled, "Jump!" I took a step forward into the unknown, and she let go of my belt. This reminded me of the leap of faith I had to take in order to fully embrace both food and my body. To my surprise, by the end of the one-hour lesson, I was doing back flips and getting caught by a trapeze artist on an opposing bar, which compares to how, farther along recovery road, I was eating intuitively and loving my body. How did these extraordinary things happen both in trapeze and in recovery? On some level, as Amelia Earhart said, "The best way to do it is to do it." People with eating disorders are so smart that we frequently come up with all kinds of creative ways around the issue at hand. For instance, we can think of numerous techniques to avoid eating, skip therapy, justify a binge, and more. Sometimes, what we really need to do is let go, stop thinking so much, and take that step—right off the trapeze platform—into freedom.

Ms. Perfectionist thrives on overthinking. Working on this tenth-year anniversary edition of *Life Without Ed*, I have been reminded again that all I can ever do is my best. When I do my best, rather than striving to do something perfectly, I am at peace. Regarding this edition of the book, perfectionism initially led me to believe that I needed to include every update and correction that I could think of, but then I realized that's a surefire way to kill a piece of art. I can't possibly go back and change my experience at the time I wrote *Life Without Ed* and also keep the integrity of the book.

I was also tempted to add technology to my story that didn't exist back then. Throughout the book I wrote about picking up the phone for help—to make a call. Well, today when people pick up the phone, it is often to send a text message. I could have easily inserted a sentence here or there that said something like, "And then I sent a text message to my friend for help." But pretending like I had a smartphone back in 2002 when I wrote the manuscript would change the authenticity of my story. I did, however, add some brief footnotes related to technology, which I hope have been helpful to you, but the fact is that no book can keep up with the ever-changing technological world. Still, always do your best to utilize the technology of your day (who knows what they will think of next) to support your recovery. Similarly, be sure to guard against the dangers. Try not to connect with people only on Facebook but nourish relationships in person as well.

In writing this afterword, I also had to realize that I cannot include everything I have learned and all that has happened since this book was released. That is, after all, why I blog (jennischaefer .com/blog) and why I have written two additional books. And, even though I don't find some of the jokes in *Life Without Ed* quite as funny as I did ten years ago, I left every single one of them intact. Because overcoming perfectionism was mandatory in order to say farewell to Ed, my goal today is to be perfectly imperfect.

"In ten years, will Ed still come around?" I asked in the first edition of this book. Well, it is ten years later, and I am happy to tell you that the answer is no. To get to this point, I never had to change Ed, but I kept changing my responses to him. Ultimately, as I described in the grocery store scene in part 7, I began to just ignore his incessant banter and, losing his power, his voice faded away. Ed and I don't even talk anymore. Back to the restaurant menu analogy: in time, I stopped ordering the "Ed Deluxe" altogether (it was no longer appealing to me), so that item was ultimately removed from the menu. A restaurant won't keep selling an entree that people aren't buying. I stopped buying into Ed, and as a quick update, so did women in my old therapy group. Like us, you can get to this place, too. The idea of a complete recovery may seem unrealistic to you, and I get that. If you are reading an electronic version of this book, do a quick search for "fully recovered" in the original text. Your result will yield a big zero. To get to where I am today—experiencing a freedom I was never quite sure existed—I had to remain open-minded (*maybe I can fully recover*) and keep walking. My hope for you is that you'll do the same.

Here's the thing: you can always go back to Ed if you decide to. Just as I was, you were born with genetic traits that made you vulnerable to having an eating disorder when in the right environment. For me, that environment had a lot to do with living in a culture that glorifies the thin ideal. Traits might include anxiety, compulsivity, and perfectionism. When I applied these traits to losing weight, I was really good at it. The same type of thing goes for you. You have the skills necessary to cultivate an eating disorder. You won't lose those skills. It's important to note that you were not born with an eating disorder but with the genetic traits that made you vulnerable. Many people have told me that they were only able to give recovery everything they had when they knew they could keep

Ed in their back pockets. This might seem contradictory to what I said previously about not keeping even the smallest part of Ed around. Let me clarify: these individuals committed to letting go of all of Ed and backed it up with solid recovery actions. Eating disordered behaviors were not an option. In the far corner of their minds, they simply knew that they could make the decision to go back to Ed someday if they wanted to. Doing this, paradoxically, was a big step in allowing them to completely remove the going-back-to-Ed idea—along with Ed—from their back pockets altogether. Only you know whether or not the idea of "keeping Ed in your back pocket" gives you permission to get better or alternatively to stay sick. I encourage you to think about this question and discuss it with your therapist. When you are recovered, my guess is that you will no longer have the desire to use your genetic traits in the service of your eating disorder but will use them to enhance your life instead. Remember what I said about applying determination to restricting Ed rather than food. That's perfectionism being used in a positive way.

Among the many magnets on my refrigerator at home hangs one with the words: "Never, never, never give up." Beneath the magnet is a rejection letter for *Life Without Ed* from a New York City literary agency. It is only one of the dozens upon dozens of rejections letters I received. They all said some version of "You're not good enough," but I knew—recovery had taught me—that I am good enough. I kept sending letters out about this book, because I knew from my personal eating disorder recovery experience that you "fall down seven times, stand up eight," which is my favorite Japanese proverb. After getting beaten up by Ed, I can say quite honesty that being rejected by New York City literary agents and publishers just wasn't that big of a deal. Eating disorder recovery builds resilience. You are resilient.

Why did that one letter make the refrigerator spot alongside my favorite calendar and family photos? Because that rejection letter is from my current literary agency. While the folks at the agency passed on this book, they were excited to work with me on my second, *Goodbye Ed, Hello Me: Recover from Your Eating Disorder and Fall in Love with Life* (jennischaefer.com/books/goodbye-ed-hello-me). If you don't quit, anything can happen. Truly, it can.

Somewhere between *Life Without Ed* and my second book, I reached what I call fully recovered—a place of laughter, relationships, dreams, passions, fun, positive body image (in a perfectly imperfect body), and, of course, inevitable life challenges like overcoming perfectionism—all concepts discussed within *Goodbye Ed, Hello Me*. Also tackled is the common question, "Who am I without Ed?" And that is another topic that you might want to explore in therapy or with a friend, alongside your thoughts on what it means to be "fully recovered." (Maybe you will choose to use different words to describe independence from your eating disorder.) It might seem as though there will be a gaping hole in your life when you kick Ed out. For a while, it can actually feel like that, but the exciting part of recovery is filling that hole up with life. When I turned in my manuscript for *Goodbye Ed, Hello Me*, I was grateful to be living in joy and peace, and, unlike before, Ed was nowhere in sight. While the topic of eating disorders has a lot to do with my professional career, my personal eating disorder is gone.

I often say that I am fully recovered from my eating disorder but not from life. I always have a lot to learn, which is a great thing because I write, speak, and sing about exactly that. I plan to utilize therapy as a tool for years to come; I have even found a great therapist here in Austin. We talk a lot about cultivating relationships and a special guy in my life—whose name is not Ed! We also discuss things like making even more room in my life for passions, including music. I fell head over heels with book writing in the process of creating *Life Without Ed*. A gift of recovery is watching how your life unfolds with dreams and desires you couldn't have even fathomed. As a kid, I used to look at books and think, "How boring; who would want to write something like that?" It turns out that I would. Since writing this book, I have focused much of my time on book-related stuff. I am beginning to understand more clearly that I won't just magically "have time" for music or anything else, but instead, I must make time. I'm working on that. Part of this process has been releasing and performing songs from my debut CD titled *phoenix, Tennessee* (jennischaefer.com/music), which refers to the mythical phoenix rising from the ashes. To my knowledge, there is no city in Tennessee named Phoenix, which is another question I get asked a lot. If you happen to have a question for me, please connect on my website, Facebook, Twitter, Google+, Pinterest, and more (see Resources in the back of this book for contact information). Obviously, I'm not too hard to find. I can't even begin to express how much I appreciate your showing interest in my work and this book.

I am thrilled to say that by the time *Life Without Ed* made it onto bookshelves about ten years ago, I was in solid recovery and on an upswing. It felt good to stand behind the words I had written (words I knew all too well after reading the book so many times). It is never too late to choose life. As I said, I had to choose recovery again—and again—and it made all of the difference. What will you choose?

For Males

"IDIDN'T FEEL like my experience as a male was much different, if at all, from those of females who were struggling with eating disorders. During my treatment, for example, I was the only male in my support group, but our experiences were strikingly similar and we related to each other very well," says Adam Lamparello, author of *Ten-Mile Morning: My Journey Through Anorexia Nervosa*. And this concept of seeking similarities rather than differences is a powerful recovery tool. There is wide agreement, according to the National Eating Disorders Association (NEDA), that eating disorders in men are clinically similar to the illness in women. In fact, also according to NEDA, males have eating disorders that are just as severe as those found in females and have similar responses to treatment. So, it makes sense that many boys and men who have recovered, like Adam, made the important decision *not* to "compare and despair" but instead to do their best to focus on what's alike in a world that still includes more eating disorder resources specifically for females than for males. Because you are reading this book, my guess is that you already know a lot about seeking similarities, and I commend you for that.

When I wrote *Life Without Ed*, it was believed that about 10 percent of people struggling with an eating disorder were men. NEDA reports that more recent research suggests that as many as one in three people with eating disorders is male. The fact is that eating disorders do not discriminate by gender, age, culture, ethnicity, sexual orientation, socioeconomic status, or anything else. Even still, some men have told me that they are afraid to seek treatment for a so-called female disease, believing it might mean that they are "weak" or "defective" in some way. But eating disorders clearly do not impact only women, as evidenced by the fact that more and more treatment centers have designed programs specifically for men. (A NEDA Navigator—see the Resources for Males at the end of this section—can help connect you with these programs.) If you are a male who is struggling, there is no shame in reaching out. In fact, there is only absolute courage in doing just that. You are strong and certainly not flawed. What you are dealing with is a life-threatening eating disorder that is all about convincing you of the opposite. Twenty-five year old Michael Elmer, who has battled both anorexia and bulimia, has said, "For every guy who seeks treatment, that's one more hero who has come forward."

One of the main reasons I added this section to *Life Without Ed* is simply to say you are not alone. Vic Avon, author of *Destroying the Monster: Lessons Learned on the Path to Recovery*, has said, "I was pretty certain that I was the only person like me." I have met countless other men who once thought they were alone and who have since found freedom. Some have spoken publicly about their experiences, and others have shared their heartfelt stories with me online or at speaking engagements. Ron Saxen, who wrote *The Good Eater: The True Story of One Man's Struggle with Binge Eating Disorder*, has helped to not only get the word out about men with eating disorders but also increase awareness of binge eating disorder. Speaker and author Troy Roness, among his other advocacy work, volunteers with Males Owning Recovery from Eating Disorders (M.O.R.E.), which is a free online support program at MentorCONNECT. Further, the inspirational stories of men as well as women are included in my latest book, *Almost Anorexic* (jennischaefer.com/books/almost-anorexic).

To strengthen your recovery and support network, consider checking out some of the resources listed at the end of this section. Many of the men I have written about here would be happy to hear from you. Also, keep reaching out to any other positive support and qualified help that you can get your hands on—even if it might be another book written by a woman. As I said, and as you may already be experiencing, finding our commonalities is what helps to set us free. Proving we are different just keeps us stuck, which I wrote about from personal experience in my second book, *Goodbye Ed, Hello Me* (jennischaefer.com/books/goodbye-ed-hello-me). Even though I was a female in treatment with lots of other females, I created a long list of how I was very "different." As long as I was adding to that list, I was not getting better. Eventually, I stopped adding to the list and even started marking things off of it. Over time, the cumulative effect of these types of pro-recovery actions is what led me to independence from Ed and to sharing my story.

I am deeply grateful to know that *Life Without Ed* has been beneficial to men as well as women over the past ten years. Whether you relate to calling your eating disorder "Ed" or not, my wish is that you have connected with the hope in my words. Some guys who have read my books have chosen to call their eating disorders by other names like Ana (short for *ana*-rexia), Mia (short for buli-*mia*), or Rex (short for ano-*rex*-ia). Regardless of what you call your eating disorder, or even if you decide not to name it at all, one thing is certain: you can get better. Full recovery is possible for everyone.

Resources for Males

NEDA Navigator
nationaleatingdisorders.org/neda-navigators

M.O.R.E.
mentorconnect-ed.org/mc_moremales

RonSaxen.com

TenMileMorning.com (Adam Lamparello)

TroyRoness.com

VicAvon.com

For Family, Friends, and Supporters

Have you ever found yourself talking to Ed trying to use common sense and logical thought? If so, you probably walked away from that conversation feeling absolutely crazy. Ed is a certifiable crazy-maker. You can't rationalize with him, and the more that you try to, the more irrational you will feel. That's the bad news. The good news is that, in order to support someone in recovery, you absolutely never need to reason with Ed. If your loved one says that Ed is screaming, "You will be a failure if you eat today," you might not understand this line of thinking at all, but you can still believe the experience as well as provide love and support.

When I e-mailed a draft of this section to my mom, she wrote back, "Dad and I still don't really understand eating disorders. But, we always did understand 'you' and completely believed what you told us and how you felt. Total support is the role of family and friends. Don't you agree?" Yes, I agree with Mom. Important to note: I wrote three books about my experience, and my parents still don't totally understand the illness. I got better anyway, and so can your loved one.

Remember you are both on the same team. Ed will do his best to make it seem as though you are in a fight against your loved one, but the battle is really with him. At times, it may seem as if the person you are supporting has literally been hijacked by Ed. In the beginning, when I was still in denial about my illness, I believed that I was my eating disorder. *It's just who I am.* I didn't have the tools to view my eating disorder as a separate entity that had control over me. When I became aware of Ed's existence, I eventually was able to acknowledge that he was, in fact, trying to take over my life, but I still felt powerless to do anything about it. Finally, with the help of health care professionals, family members, and friends, I was ready to do absolutely everything possible to break free.

At presentations that I give across the globe, I sometimes act out the chair scene from the opening pages of *Life Without Ed*. This describes the first time in therapy when I separated from Ed, put him in a chair, and had a dialogue back and forth. I often ask audience members, "What's in your chair?" Whether we have an eating disorder or not, we all have something in our chair. No one is immune from self-criticism. How does your negative voice make you feel? Now, imagine hearing that voice constantly—even in your dreams at night. This is just a glimpse of what it can be like to have an eating disorder. Because Ed was so noisy in my life, I needed the voices of support around me to be firm, constant, and turned up a notch in volume. (I am talking about loud in metaphorical decibels.)

Finding the right words is difficult but possible. As explained in the "Impurities" section of this book, the Ed filter will attempt to contaminate your well-intentioned words. In general, if you don't know what to say, try things like, "It will get better," "I believe in you," and "I love you." Some people with eating disorders may find it supportive for their friends and family members to remind them to separate from Ed by saying, "Who's talking right now— Ed or you?" Others will find this kind of questioning absolutely annoying and counterproductive. So, you will need to ask, "What feels supportive?" as well as, "What doesn't?" Keep in mind that these answers will change over time. Early on in my recovery, I often wanted to talk with my family specifically about food and related behaviors. After keeping everything inside for so long, it was such a relief to reveal the secrets of my disorder. But, ultimately, when I was well connected with treatment providers and my therapy group, I didn't want to discuss food with my family as much; instead, I wanted to connect with them about my life beyond Ed. I have met families who have found it helpful to specify certain times of the day or week to talk about (and to not talk about) Ed. When a child suffering with an eating disorder still lives at home, parents sometimes have no other option than to discuss eating. In these cases, some have found it beneficial to ask their child, "What is the most supportive way for us to speak with you about food?"

What else can you do?

- **Model balanced eating behaviors and positive body image as well as self-care and self-compassion.** Think of a flight attendant's instructions just before takeoff: "Put your oxygen mask on first before assisting others." Related to eating disorders, this means get support for yourself in order to be at your best for your loved one. Connect with the National Eating Disorders Association's Parent, Family, and Friends Network (PFN) at nationaleatingdisorders.org/parent-family-friends-network. Join an online discussion with Families Empowered and Supporting Treatment of Eating Disorders (F.E.A.S.T.) at feast-ed.org. If your partner struggles with an eating disorder, learn about Uniting Couples in the Treatment of Anorexia Nervosa (UCAN) at unceatingdisorders.org/ucan.

- **Assist your loved one in receiving continual, qualified care.** Seek professional help and get diverse opinions, asking providers if they incorporate evidence-based approaches (family-based treatment for anorexia and cognitive-behavioral therapy for bulimia and EDNOS), which have significant scientific support. Always keep in mind that there is more than one way to treat an eating disorder; each person needs a very individualized treatment plan. Make sure that nutritional support is a part of any program. Food is, after all, the best medicine. For guidance in finding help, the NEDA Navigators program (nationaleatingdisorders.org/neda-navigators), which is part of the PFN Network mentioned earlier, can connect you with a trained volunteer who has experience in fighting Ed.

- **Connect your loved one with someone who is recovered from an eating disorder.** (The NEDA Navigators program can help with this, too.) In addition to being an inspiration, a recovered person is in a unique position to be more direct about certain critical issues. For instance, "just eat" can feel condescending and unsupportive coming from someone who has never had an eating disorder. But, as I wrote about in *Goodbye Ed, Hello Me* (jennischaefer.com/books/goodbye-ed-hello-me), these two words—when spoken by those who have been there—can actually motivate. When the women in my therapy group eventually told me to "just eat," I listened and moved toward more fully embracing food.
- **Do not blame yourself.** My parents didn't cause my eating disorder, but they did absolutely everything they could to help me get better. Releasing guilt and blame will put you in a better position to assist your loved one. Learning about the genetic link to eating disorders can be helpful in this pursuit. As discussed in my latest book, *Almost Anorexic* (jennischaefer.com/books/almost-anorexic), research suggests that 50 to 80 percent of eating disorder risk is due to genetic effects.
- **Keep learning.** Read books similar to this one that can provide a window into the mind of someone with an eating disorder. If you and your loved one relate to my experience, you may want to check out my other two books. There are also informative ones written specifically for family and friends.

I never would have recovered without the help of my amazing family and friends. I lost hope a lot. They never did. At some points, it seemed as though we were running a relay race—a marathon rather than a sprint—where I could hand off my baton when I got tired. I passed it to my mom, dad, brothers, and friends. No matter what happened, regardless of how many times I fell down, they kept saying, "You can do it." And I finally finished the race. Full recovery from an eating disorder is possible. It is important to note that there was no specific day when I crossed the finish line into complete independence from Ed, but hindsight really is twenty-twenty. By looking back over my life and reflecting years after the fact, I saw that I was recovered. My family noticed first, saying, "Wow, Jenni! You really are better." Today, the words *Ed* and *eating disorder* are not a part of our conversation—unless we are talking about one of my books. Yes, it gets that good. My family is healthier, happier, and stronger than ever before. You can get there, too.

An Exercise Idea to Discuss with Your Loved One

Many people with eating disorders have told me that it was beneficial for them to read this book, highlight parts they particularly related to, and then pass along the marked-up copy to their family member or friend. In this way, you will gain not only the knowledge from my personal experience but also a clearer understanding of how your loved one does and doesn't relate to my story. Others have preferred to simply read the book out loud together, taking turns reading a short section each morning or night.

For Treatment Professionals

I DIDN'T ACKNOWLEDGE the voice of Ed in my own life until people like you said, "Jenni, you don't have to listen anymore." In this way, you gave me a voice. You have empowered countless people not only to find their voices but to reclaim their lives. Even though you might not hear back personally over the years from every single person who has ever walked through your door, one thing is for sure: you are a significant factor behind many diplomas, marriages, friendships, partnerships, births, and other exciting things. What you do makes a difference—thank you.

Over the past decade, numerous therapists, dietitians, doctors, and other treatment professionals have shared insights with me about how they incorporate *Life Without Ed* into their practices. Those personally touched by eating disorders have also connected with me regarding how their treatment teams used this book to help them. Since I am not in the trenches day-to-day working with those who struggle, it only makes sense for me to pass this wisdom along to you. I hope that you will find some of the concepts, tools, and exercises listed here useful in your work. Of course, many of these ideas can be applied to other positive, recovery-oriented books as well.

1. Separate from the Eating Disorder

Long before *Life Without Ed* was released, clinicians across the globe had been using the concept of separating the illness from the person. In the *Treatment Manual for Anorexia Nervosa: A Family-Based Approach*, psychiatrist James Lock and his colleagues suggest that "By stressing that AN [anorexia nervosa] is not identical to the patient herself, the therapist can emphasize the support for the developing adolescent, while at the same time distinguishing AN as a problem the patient has. This strategy is key in maintaining engagement with the adolescent while attacking AN." From what I have been told, *Life Without Ed* helped to make this idea even more usable and clear for some clients. Much of this book was written specifically to aid in separating a person's identity from that of the eating disorder. To make this split, which can be incredibly beneficial early on in recovery, many clinicians have an "Ed chair" in their office and have encouraged some clients to designate one at home as well. As an activity, patients in treatment programs have decorated an Ed chair together to remind themselves to make some room for their own unique personalities. Dialoging with Ed, which is illustrated throughout this book and as a specific exercise in part 4, has been quite effective in helping people to separate from their illness. In the early days of my recovery, writing conversations with Ed allowed me to direct anger that had been pointed at myself toward the eating disorder instead. Further along my journey, as mentioned in the afterword, I stopped fighting against Ed so much and began focusing more on cultivating self-love and self-compassion.

2. Don't Blame Ed, and More on Separation

"Of course, my eating disorder was never really a guy named Ed who followed me around night and day, but it sure felt like it. Ed stood for a collection of beliefs I had learned since I was born. Unlike other recovery models, I learned that Ed was not an aspect of my authentic self, so my goal was always to separate from him. Different recovery models and tools work better for different people," I explained in *Goodbye Ed, Hello Me* (jennischaefer.com/books/goodbye-ed-hello-me). I also discussed in that book (and in the afterword to this book) a crucial point regarding Ed and accountability that was first brought to my attention by licensed marriage and family therapist Carolyn Costin, author of *Your Diet-*

ing Daughter, among others. Thanks to Carolyn, "don't blame Ed" is now a significant part of my work. One of the fundamental reasons to separate from Ed is to put oneself in a position to make pro-recovery decisions and actions—not to use the excuse, "Ed made me do it."

3. Separate from Ms. Perfectionist and Other Voices

This externalization technique has been applied to perfectionism ("Ms. Perfectionist"), alcoholism ("Al"), and nicotine ("Nic"). Over the years, people have also shared their personal stories with me about "Addy," which stands for addiction. Recently at speaking events, I have discussed Ani (pronounced "Annie"), which stands for that "*anti*-relationship" part of me that used to fight really hard to stay isolated and alone. As you know, people with eating disorders are super creative and can come up with innovative names when prompted. Some individuals even use separation tools and exercises with OCD (obsessive-compulsive disorder) and PTSD (post-traumatic stress disorder). Many have had conversations with "Mr. OCD," for instance.

4. Break Through Denial and Reach Acceptance

I have been happy to learn how *Life Without Ed* has been used to help some people break through denial. Apparently, it is difficult for someone to deny that they have an eating disorder when they read about Ed and realize that they have a lot of the same thoughts. Many recognize that what they originally believed was just a "peculiarity" or "quirk" in their own eating is actually the same exact behavior that I reference in regard to a life-threatening illness. Licensed clinical social worker Susie Hair has suggested that clients read the section "Ed's Rules" in part 1 to assist them in accepting that they do, in fact, have an eating disorder. She explained, "I will also ask my clients to make a list of all of Ed's rules for themselves.

If they do not believe they have an eating disorder, I ask them to make a list of their personal rules around food, weight, and size. This too is an eye-opener that slowly helps to pull them out of denial. Their list helps them realize they are not in control; Ed is." Some professionals have asked their clients to take a highlighter or pen to *Life Without Ed*—identifying any and all words that they connect with. A heavily marked-up book can be a powerful visual.

5. Stay Motivated

Early in recovery, you may ask your clients to consider the pros and cons of the eating disorder in order to enhance motivation for change. Certainly, Ed's promises (e.g., "You'll feel great about yourself if you drop pounds!") will feel like pros. But, as the clinician, you can gently guide your clients to appreciate that Ed's verbal and physical abuse is a pretty big con. The "Good and Bad About Ed" exercise in part 6 explores this concept. Later in treatment, when someone hits a rough patch and fears they are sliding backward, here's a unique approach: imagine what it would be like for a client who feels discouraged to read a book that points out specific progress through his or her own experience—not mine or another author's. That is just what some professionals have done by asking clients, in early recovery, to highlight this book as mentioned in number 4 and then, later on, asking them to reread it for motivation. When these individuals reread the book, taking particular note of the words that they had marked in their first days of trying to get better, they start to see just how far they have actually traveled along recovery road. Some professionals have asked clients to write notes about their thoughts and feelings in the book as well. Men and women in recovery have e-mailed me saying that, through this exercise, they were amazed to see how much progress they had made. On a second pass through *Life Without Ed*, they could no longer relate as much (or at all) to their original highlights and notes.

6. Show There Is Hope

Life Without Ed is often recommended simply to demonstrate that recovery is possible. Some professionals, then, use my next book, *Goodbye Ed, Hello Me*, to go a step further and show that "fully recovered" can be a reality as well. People suffering with eating disorders as well as their families often believe that no one ever gets better. This makes sense, as many have never met anyone who is recovered. So my story and that of others can be living proof that full recovery is within reach. Naturally, some people struggling with eating disorders won't believe my story at first. (I wouldn't have either!) It can, therefore, be essential to connect them with more than just one hopeful book or story. My latest book, *Almost Anorexic*, includes the recovery journeys of a wide array of people, particularly those with subclinical illness who mistakenly believe that they don't deserve or need help. Further, my website blog shares the stories of others who have recovered from eating disorders and overcome adversity. (Just click on the "Dream Big" category at jennischaefer.com/blog.) With lots of examples, people often begin to believe. I know that I did, albeit slowly at first.

7. Use as a Recovery Companion

In today's digital world, some professionals have recommended the e-book version of *Life Without Ed*. The audio book can be helpful as well. Then, clients can carry positive words with them wherever they go—even on their smartphones. People with eating disorders have told me that it is extremely useful to essentially have recovery in their pocket, accessible at a moment's notice in tough situations. This recovery companion can be especially beneficial if you are asking your clients to use "urge surfing" or delay tactics such as "when you feel the urge to binge, wait 10 minutes before allowing yourself to act on it." It goes without saying that this idea can be applied to other books, too—not just mine.

8. Harness the Power of Music

Some clinicians have played the song in the back of this book, also titled "Life Without Ed," in therapy sessions as a basis for discussion. You and your client can listen to the entire song for free on my website (jennischaefer.com/music). It is also available on my CD, *phoenix, Tennessee*, which includes other motivational songs like "She Blames Herself," an account of overcoming sexual abuse. For some, the power of music in healing cannot be underestimated. Many people benefit from making a recovery music playlist on their smartphone or MP3 player. A playlist can be created to last a specific amount of time (for example, ten minutes) to support that binge delay tactic mentioned earlier. In general, inspirational music playing in the car can help some people to resist turning into that drive-thru to binge. Those who battle compulsive exercise have found it helpful to create a playlist to last the number of minutes prescribed by their physician for working out. When the playlist is over, exercise should be, too.

9. Use in Group Therapy

Life Without Ed has served as the basis for numerous groups. Here is a list of ideas:

- Incorporate downloadable discussion questions from my website that were created specifically for each of my books (jennischaefer.com/discuss).
- Read one short section from the book as the basis for each group session.
- Use a specific therapeutic exercise as a group activity, such as writing and then sharing your own "Declaration of Independence from Ed."
- Ask one group member to read a short section aloud, and use that theme as a check-in for everyone.

- Listen to the song "Life Without Ed" and discuss. Ask group members to bring other positive, uplifting songs to share.

10. Support Loved Ones

Many professionals ask loved ones to read this book to help them "get into the mind" of someone with an eating disorder. Friends and family members can gain not only much hope but also critical insight into just how insidious an eating disorder can be. My story makes it clear that the illness is not "just a phase." Reading *Life Without Ed* can also be a good way for loved ones to begin to see the eating disorder as separate from the person who struggles. Everyone can then be on the same team fighting against Ed. I added the "For Family, Friends, and Supporters" section to this book specifically as a tool to guide parents, spouses, siblings, teachers, partners, friends, and others. In addition to asking loved ones to read this book for themselves, some professionals have also suggested that the person struggling with the eating disorder read certain sections and then discuss the topic with their parents or friends. Also, note the exercise idea, written for family members to use, on page 207.

11. Train Other Professionals

Life Without Ed is required reading in many treatment programs for staff. It is quite an honor (not to mention, a surprise) to know that my words and thoughts as a twenty-something are being used as a teaching tool to help professionals gain a better understanding of just how an eating disorder can manifest in someone's mind. Clinical psychologist Michael E. Berrett, coauthor of *Spiritual Approaches in the Treatment of Women with Eating Disorders,* has said, "Each section in *Life Without Ed* includes nuggets of clinical wisdom. The dialogue between Jenni and her treatment team is useful in helping professionals to both learn more about the underpinnings of the illness as well as to ignite new ideas to utilize with their own clients in sessions." I certainly didn't plan on any of this when I wrote the book, but I am grateful that it worked out that way.

12. Go-to Short Sections and Exercises

I wrote *Life Without Ed* so that it doesn't have to be read in any particular order. Therefore, rather than assigning the entire book to a client, which can feel overwhelming, stand alone sections can be utilized to target current recovery goals. When accompanied by journaling and thorough follow-up in therapy, one or two short sections can make a big impact. The book is divided into seven parts that range in topics from separating the person from the illness (part 1) and facing the food (part 2) to improving negative body image (part 3) and the nuts and bolts of recovery (part 4). While parts 5 and 6 can provide support in overcoming relapse, part 7 is all about hope and motivation. The various exercises within the book can obviously be used as individual assignments as well. The *Life Without Ed* page of my website (jennischaefer.com/books/life-without-ed) includes downloadable exercises and additional resources, including an online compulsive exercise test backed by research.

• • •

Whether you are a professional who has been required to read this book or one who chose to do so on your own, thank you. I would not be able to do what I do (and love) without your support. As a matter of fact, a lot of people wouldn't be able to do what they do—truly live—without your efforts. Of course, there will always be that one who isn't too happy with you: Ed certainly wishes that you would retire early. You've caused way too many divorces in his life. Keep up the great work!

Divorce Decree from Ed

In the court of recovered rocks, _____, _____,
_____(City)_____(State/Province/Region)

_____, **Plaintiff**
(Your Name)

vs.   **Case ID:**
Ed, Defendant   UCanDoIt!

This cause came on for hearing on _____ (insert date)
upon the complaint of the Plaintiff, and upon consideration thereof, the
Court enters judgment as hereinafter set forth.

The Court finds that the parties were married on _____
(insert date). The Court also finds that the parties are incompatible and
that the Plaintiff is entitled to a divorce as demanded.

Grounds for Divorce

1. Ed is abusive, controlling, and manipulative.
2. _____
3. _____

Allocation of Parental Rights

No children have been born. Therefore, no communication is necessary
between the parties. This means that full recovery is possible!

Property Division

IT IS ORDERED, ADJUDGED, AND DECREED that the parties' marital property
and debt be distributed between the parties as follows:

Ed can take back his pain, misery, lies, and _____.

Plaintiff is entitled to all happiness, laughter, dreams, relationships, and love.
(Below, write recovery gifts in your life.)

_____

_____

Signed

Plaintiff _____ Date _____

Supporters of This Divorce

Jenni Schaefer

Downloadable "Divorce Decree from Ed" available at jennischaefer.com/divorce.

"Life Without Ed"

Words and music written by Jenni Schaefer and Judy Rodman

I was chasing down the image for so long
Of that perfect girl that I just had to be.
She was never quite the one I saw,
How I let that dreadful mirror torture me.

It was killing me to try to look like her,
The amazing woman who could turn each head.
I was losing so much more than all the weight.
My very heart and soul were left unfed.

I called the monster Ed.
He so controlled my head,
Until a greater power spoke the truth—it said.

Chorus:

Life without Ed is waiting here for you.
Be strong, keep the faith and you'll see it coming true.
You don't have to just pretend,
All the pain can really end.
You deserve more than the lies you've been fed.
You can believe in life without Ed.

So I listened to the wisdom sent my way,
And I let the long awakening begin.
I have found such freedom I can truly say
That the image in the mirror is my friend.

I called the monster Ed.
He so controlled my head,
Until a greater power spoke the truth—it said.

REPEAT CHORUS

BRIDGE:

When the chains that bind your freedom are so strong,
When you think there is no way you can go on,
Cause you've tried and you've failed to break away,
Look at me and see someone who can say.

REPEAT CHORUS

If you would like to listen to this song or to learn more about Jenni's music, visit jennischaefer.com/music or check out her CD, *phoenix, Tennessee*. To learn more about Judy Rodman, Jenni's vocal coach and the co-writer of this song, visit judyrodman.com.

Jenni Schaefer

phoenix, Tennessee

Resources

The following list includes only a small sample of what is available. For further resources, visit jennischaefer.com.

Get Help—Advocacy Organizations

National Eating Disorders Association (NEDA)
myneda.org
Chat online with a trained volunteer, or call the Helpline at 1-800-931-2237. Find local resources and support.

Academy for Eating Disorders (AED)
aedweb.org

Beating Eating Disorders (Beat)
b-eat.co.uk (United Kingdom)

Binge Eating Disorder Association (BEDA)
bedaonline.com

Butterfly Foundation for Eating Disorders
thebutterflyfoundation.org.au (Australia)

Eating Disorder Hope
eatingdisorderhope.com

Families Empowered and Supporting Treatment of Eating Disorders (F.E.A.S.T.)
feast-ed.org

FINDING*balance*
findingbalance.com

International Association of Eating Disorders Professionals Foundation (iaedp)
iaedp.com

Multi-Service Eating Disorders Association, Inc. (MEDA)
medainc.org

National Eating Disorder Information Centre (NEDIC)
nedic.ca (Canada)

National Eating Disorders Collaboration (NEDC)
nedc.com.au (Australia)

Connect with Others—Free Support

Eating Disorders Anonymous—Twelve-Step Meetings
eatingdisordersanonymous.org

MentorCONNECT—Global Mentoring Community
mentorconnect-ed.org

National Association of Anorexia Nervosa and Associated Disorders (ANAD)—Support Groups
anad.org

Something Fishy—Online Support
something-fishy.org

Help with Paying for Treatment

NEDA's Insurance Resources
myneda.org/insurance-resources

EDReferral.com—Alternative Payment Ideas
edreferral.com/research.htm

F.R.E.E.D. Foundation (For Recovery and Elimination of Eating Disorders)—Scholarships
freedfoundation.org

Kirsten Haglund Foundation—Scholarships
kirstenhaglund.org

Manna Fund—Scholarships
mannafund.org

Project HEAL (Help to Eat, Accept and Live)—Scholarships
theprojectheal.org

Learn More About Jenni's Work

JenniSchaefer.com
Listen to music, read articles and frequently asked questions, download recovery tools, and watch Jenni's speaking reel as well as other videos. Check out her calendar of events; she would love to meet you. Join her e-newsletter for inspiration in your in-box!

Jenni's Blog
jennischaefer.com/blog

Jenni's Books
jennischaefer.com/books

Almost Anorexic with Harvard Medical School
almostanorexic.com

Dream Big—Share *Your* Story
jennischaefer.com/dream-big

Ed Jewelry
sarah-kate.com

Recovered.® Store
recoveredstore.com

Connect with Jenni—Social Media

Facebook.com/LifeWithoutEd
Jenni does her best to respond to each and every message posted on her Timeline.

Goodreads.com/JenniSchaefer
Join a community of people who love books.

Google.com/+JenniSchaefer
Jenni makes an effort to respond personally to each message posted on her page.

LinkedIn.com/in/JenniSchaefer
Learn more about Jenni's work on this network for professionals.

Pinterest.com/JenniSchaeferTX
Check out videos, music, articles, and more.

Twitter.com/JenniSchaefer
Stay connected with information about recovery and fulfilled living.

About the Authors

JENNI SCHAEFER is a singer/songwriter and author living in Austin, Texas. Her books include *Goodbye Ed, Hello Me* and *Almost Anorexic*. For more information about Jenni, her music, and her availability as a speaker/performer, visit her website: jennischaefer.com.

THOM RUTLEDGE is a psychotherapist and author of several books, including *Embracing Fear: How to Turn What Scares Us into Our Greatest Gift*. For more information, visit his website: thomrutledge.com.